Reading Through History

Oklahoma History

1907 through Present

By Jake Henderson & Robert Marshall

Oklahoma History
1907 through Present
(Student Edition)
by Jake Henderson & Robert Marshall
©2015

ISBN-13: 978-1512272840

ISBN-10: 1512272841

Please visit our sites at
https://www.facebook.com/ReadingThroughHistory
http://readingthroughhistory.com

Table of Contents:

Unit One:
1910s & 1920s

Jim Thorpe

Jim Thorpe was one of the most legendary athletes who ever lived. Who was Jim Thorpe? What did he do to become so famous?

In 1888, just outside of Prague, Oklahoma, twins were born to Hiram and Charlotte Thorpe. The young couple named their two sons Charlie and Jim. The two boys were raised as members of the Sac and Fox tribe, but their parents had a diverse ethnic background. The Kickapoo and Potawatomie tribes were represented in their family history, as well as Irish and French ancestors.

Jim's early years were fairly typical. He enjoyed hunting and fishing, he went to school, and he helped his father on the farm. Sadly, when the twin boys were nine, Charlie contracted pneumonia and lost his life. Despite the loss of his brother, Jim tried to continue going to school, but he was not a good student and he disliked being confined to a classroom.

Words to watch for:

confined   practical

decathlon   prowess

He was sent away to more than one boarding school, including the Haskell Institute in Lawrence, Kansas, as well as the Carlisle Indian Industrial School in Carlisle, Pennsylvania. Carlisle was a well-known school for Native Americans. The school required students to speak English, rather than their native languages, and taught strong discipline and practical work skills.

While attending Carlisle, Thorpe became a standout track and field star. By the end of his first season on the track team, he had set every school record. He once won six events in the same meet, defeating the other team single-handedly! Aside from his track abilities, Jim participated in many other sports at Carlisle. He played basketball, lacrosse, tennis, hockey, and handball. He also participated in swimming, gymnastics, rowing, and ice skating. He even won the intercollegiate ballroom dancing championship in 1912!

However, Jim was not satisfied. He wanted to play football. The Carlisle School had one of the best football teams in the country. They were coached by the legendary Glenn "Pop" Warner. At first, Warner was hesitant to let the school's track star play football. However, Jim dazzled the coach with an impressive tryout. He evaded all of Carlisle's defenders multiple times. At the end of his tryout, Jim tossed the football to Warner and said, "Nobody is going to tackle Jim."

While playing for the Carlisle Indians, Jim Thorpe became the team's best player. He played running back, defensive back, kicker, and punter. During the 1912 season, he scored 25 touchdowns and led Carlisle to the 1912 national collegiate championship.

That same year, Thorpe participated in the Summer Olympics in Stockholm, Sweden. He competed in the pentathlon and the decathlon, as well as the high jump and long jump. He won gold medals in both the pentathlon and decathlon.

The King of Sweden, Gustav V, presented the gold medals to Thorpe. When he did so, he looked at the young athlete and remarked, "You, sir, are the greatest athlete in the world." Jim's only reply was, "Thanks, King."

Unfortunately, six months later it was discovered that Jim had played baseball earlier in his life and had received a small amount of money to do so. In the eyes of the International Olympic Committee, this made him a professional athlete. At the time, only amateur athletes could participate in the Olympics. As a result, the IOC stripped Thorpe of his gold medals and removed his name from the record books.

This did not stop Thorpe's athletic career, however. He would continue participating in professional sports until the age of 41. He played professional baseball and football, as well as having very brief career in basketball. Following his playing career, he struggled with poverty and failing health. He eventually died in 1953, at the age of 64. Twenty years after his death, it was decided to restore his name to the Olympic record book, and his gold medals were returned to his family.

Thorpe's prowess as an athlete is legendary. In 2000, the Associated Press voted him the #2 athlete of the century, behind only Babe Ruth. ABC Sports took a similar poll and ranked him #1, ahead of Muhammad Ali, Jesse Owens, and Michael Jordan! He has been honored in numerous other ways. He is in the National Football Hall of Fame, there are numerous buildings and awards which bear his name, and there is even a town named in his honor.

Multiple Choice: *Select the choice that completes the statement or answers the question.*

1._____ Which of the following best describes the Carlisle Indian Industrial School?
a. This school helped Native American students get in touch with their tribal roots.
b. This school required students to speak English and taught practical work skills.
c. This school specialized in teaching young Native Americans about other cultures.
d. This school taught Native Americans how to cook, clean, and drive automobiles.

2._____ Which of the following best summarizes Jim Thorpe's athletic career at Carlisle?
a. He was a standout star in track, football, and virtually every other sport imaginable.
b. He played football exceptionally well, but did not participate in other sports.
c. He was an exceptional track athlete, but was prevented from playing other sports because he was Native American.
d. He played baseball and basketball, but was not that talented at the other major sports.

3._____ Which of the following statements was made about Jim Thorpe?
a. "There is no doubt, you are the fastest man alive."
b. "He's the only man I've ever met that I didn't like."
c. "You can do anything you set your mind to."
d. "You, sir, are the greatest athlete in the world."

4._____ Which of the following best explains why Jim Thorpe had his Olympic medals taken from him?
a. It was discovered that he had used performance enhancing steroids.
b. It was discovered that he had placed a wager on himself.
c. It was discovered that he had been paid to play baseball.
d. It was discovered that he was not actually an American citizen.

5._____ Which of the following statements about Jim Thorpe is *not* accurate?
a. An ABC Sports poll ranked him as the #1 athlete of the century.
b. His Olympic medals have yet to be returned to his family.
c. He is in the National Football Hall of Fame.
d. There are numerous buildings and awards which bear his name.

Vocabulary: *Match each word with its correct definition. Consider how the word is used in the lesson. This might help you define each term. Use a dictionary to help if necessary.*

a. confined   d. poverty
b. practical   e. prowess
c. decathlon

6._____ unable to leave a place

7._____ an athletic contest made up of ten different events

8._____ exceptional or superior ability

9._____ useful for actual work and everyday life

10._____ the condition of having little or no money

Guided Reading: *Fill in the blanks below to create complete sentences.*

1. Jim Thorpe was sent away to more than one boarding school, including the _____ Institute in Lawrence, Kansas.

2. While attending Carlisle, Thorpe became a standout _____ star.

3. The Carlisle School had one of the best _____ teams in the country.

4. While playing for the Carlisle Indians, Jim Thorpe became the team's best player, playing _____, defensive back, kicker, and punter.

5. At the Summer Olympics, Thorpe competed in the pentathlon and the _____.

6. The IOC stripped Thorpe of his gold medals and removed his name from the _____.

7. Thorpe played professional _____ and football, as well as having a very brief career in basketball.

8. Following his playing career, Thorpe struggled with poverty and failing _____.

9. In 2000, the Associated Press voted him the #2 athlete of the century, behind only _____.

10. There is even a _____ named in Jim Thorpe's honor.

Summarize: *Answer the following questions in the space provided. Attempt to respond in a complete sentence for each question. Be sure to use correct capitalization and punctuation!*

1. Who was Jim Thorpe's football coach at Carlisle?

2. What events did Thorpe compete in at the Summer Olympics?

3. When did Carlisle win the national collegiate championship in football?

4. Where was the Summer Olympics that Thorpe participated in?

5. Why did the Carlisle football coach not want Thorpe to play football?

6. How did playing baseball result in Thorpe having his Olympic medals taken away?

Student Response: *Write a paragraph addressing the questions raised below. A thorough response should consist of three to five complete sentences.*

7. How do you feel Jim Thorpe would compare to today's modern superstar athletes? Explain your answer as thoroughly as possible.

Green Corn Rebellion

An incident occurred in 1917 that became known as the Green Corn Rebellion. What was the Green Corn Rebellion? How did this event come to an end?

In 1917, the United States made the decision to enter World War I. On May 18th, 1917, Congress passed a law imposing military conscription. As a result, all eligible young men in the United States were required to register for the draft on June 5th, 1917.

Numbers being selected for the draft

There were many opponents to America's participation in the war. One of the strongest detractors was the Socialist Party of America. The Socialist Party held rallies, gave speeches, and printed pamphlets about why the United States should not become involved in the war.

The Socialist Party had always had a strong presence in the state of Oklahoma. There were many poor farmers who sympathized with socialist theories of redistributing wealth to improve their lives. In fact, a socialist organization known as the Working Class Union claimed to have as many as 35,000 members in the state of Oklahoma. This organization was highly opposed to conscription and used their influence in Oklahoma to agitate the situation.

Rural farmers who opposed conscription felt that it was a violation of their rights. Therefore, they planned to rebel against the government for attempting to take their sons away to fight and die in a far off land. On August 3rd, 1917, an armed group of nearly 1,000 poor farmers met on the banks of the South Canadian River, near Ada, Oklahoma.

> **Words to watch for:**
>
> conscription   socialist
>
> repeal   vigilantes

They planned to march all the way to Washington D.C. Their hope was that, as they marched, other likeminded individuals would join them and swell their ranks to thousands. When the group arrived in Washington D.C., they would overthrow the government, repeal the draft, and end America's involvement in the war. As they marched, they planned on living off of roasted green corn and barbecued beef.

Before the march even began, a posse of vigilantes met the rebels on the banks of the river. When the farmers saw the posse approaching they scattered in disorder. Only hours after the rebellion had begun, it came to an abrupt end. Three died during the short-lived violence and nearly 450 were arrested. Most of these were eventually released, but 150 of the revolutionaries were charged with crimes and sentenced to prison.

The Green Corn Rebellion signaled the end of the strong socialist presence in Oklahoma. Many saw the Socialist Party as responsible for the incident, and its popularity in the state quickly waned.

Multiple Choice: *Select the choice that completes the statement or answers the question.*

1._____ Which of the following was the Socialist Party of America strongly opposed
   to in 1917?
a. They were strongly opposed to the United States becoming involved in World War I.
b. They were strongly opposed to the United States abandoning the gold standard.
c. They were strongly opposed to women gaining the right to vote.
d. They were strongly opposed to the prohibition movement.

2._____ Why did many farmers sympathize with socialists in Oklahoma?
a. Many farmers were poor and agreed with socialist theories of wealth redistribution.
b. Most farmers were opposed to the idea of women voting.
c. Many farmers were opposed to the idea of prohibition.
d. Most farmers supported the gold standard, so favored the socialist position on this issue.

3._____ Which of the following best explains why farmers were planning on rebelling?
a. They felt that taxes were too high and that the government was stealing money from them.
b. They did not want their beef and produce being sold to foreign dictators.
c. They felt that they were not being fairly represented in congress.
d. They did not want their sons to fight and die in a far off land.

4._____ Which of the following best summarizes the plan for the Green Corn Rebellion?
a. Farmers would march to Washington D.C., burning corn fields as they marched.
b. Farmers would march to Green Corn, Pennsylvania, where a major rally was planned.
c. Farmers would march to Washington D.C., living off of green corn as they traveled.
d. Farmers would march to New York City, refusing to supply any more corn for the war effort.

5._____ Which of the following best describes how the Green Corn Rebellion came to an end?
a. The farmers arrived in Washington D.C. and fought a battle against National Guard troops.
b. A posse of vigilantes met the rebel farmers and the marchers scattered in disorder.
c. Thousands set out to Washington D.C., but most lost interest and went home before they
   reached their goal.
d. The farmers arrived in Washington D.C. where they were greeted by the president who
   listened to their grievances.

Vocabulary: *Match each word with its correct definition. Consider how the word is used in the lesson. This might help you define each term. Use a dictionary to help if necessary.*

a. conscription
b. sympathize
c. socialist
d. Repeal
e. Vigilante

6._____ one who supports the equal redistribution of wealth and opposes
   private ownership of businesses

7._____ one who takes the enforcement of law into their own hands

8._____ to officially revoke or remove

9._____ mandatory enrollment into military service; a draft

10._____ to share the feeling of another

Guided Reading: *Fill in the blanks below to create complete sentences.*

1. All eligible young men in the United States were required to register for the
_____ on June 5th, 1917.

2. The Socialist Party held rallies, gave speeches, and printed _____
about why the United States should not become involved in the war.

3. A socialist organization known as the Working Class Union claimed to have as many
as _____ members in the state of Oklahoma.

4. Their hope was that, as they marched, other likeminded individuals would join them
and swell their ranks to _____.

5. The Green Corn Rebellion signaled the end of the strong _____
presence in Oklahoma.

Correct the Statement: *Each of the following sentences is false. Circle the incorrect word and write the word or phrase that makes the statement correct in the answer blank provided.*

6. One of the strongest detractors of America's entry into World War I was the
Democrat Party of America. _____

7. The Working Class Union was highly opposed to conscription and used their
influence in Texas to agitate the situation. _____

8. On August 3rd, 1917, an armed group of nearly 1,000 poor farmers met on the banks
of the South Arkansas River. _____

9. When the group arrived in Washington D.C., they planned to overthrow the media,
repeal the draft, and end America's involvement in the war. _____

10. 150 of the bystanders were charged with crimes and sentenced to prison.
_____

Summarize: *Answer the following questions in the space provided. Attempt to respond in a complete sentence for each question. Be sure to use correct capitalization and punctuation!*

1. Who passed a law imposing military conscription?

2. What was the hope of those who planned on marching?

3. When did the Green Corn Rebellion begin?

4. Where were the marchers planning on marching to?

5. Why did rural farmers oppose conscription?

6. How were the marchers planning on living as they marched?

Student Response: *Write a paragraph addressing the questions raised below. A thorough response should consist of three to five complete sentences.*

7. Those who marched in the Green Corn Rebellion had the intention of overthrowing the government. Do you think such an effort would ever be successful? Why or why not? Explain your answer as thoroughly as possible.

Frank Phillips

Frank Phillips became one of the wealthiest men who ever lived in Oklahoma. Who was Frank Phillips? How did he become so successful?

In 1874, Frank Phillips was born in Scotia, Nebraska. That same year, a swarm of grasshoppers wiped out his father's crops. As a result, the Phillips family moved to Iowa, where Frank and his ten brothers and sisters were raised.

Phillips became an apprentice barber at the age of 14, and by the time he was 24, he owned three barbershops. He married Jane Gibson, whose father was the president of a bank. John Gibson convinced Frank to join him in selling savings bonds.

One day in 1903, while on a business trip to St. Louis, Phillips met an old friend who told him about the oil that could be found in the Osage Nation, in Indian Territory. Later that year, Phillips and his younger brother organized the Anchor Oil & Gas Company. The brothers became what were known as wildcatters. A wildcatter was someone who drilled for oil in areas not known for producing oil.

The company drilled its first well in 1905, striking oil on June 23rd. Their second and third wells were dry. They had little money left, but made the decision to drill a fourth well. The fourth well was completed on September 16, 1905 and proved to be a gusher. They earned more than $100,000 from this well, and it became the first of more than 80 wells in a row which were successful for the brothers.

Words to watch for:
bonds wildcatter
gusher consolidate

However, it wasn't until World War I when Phillips experienced his biggest success. As the United States became more involved in the war, oil prices continued to go up. As the prices continued to climb, the brothers decided to consolidate their holdings into one company, Phillips Petroleum. This new company was created on June 13, 1917.

Frank Phillips headed Phillips Petroleum for 22 years before finally retiring in 1939. In the year of his retirement as president, the company made $24 million in profit. Phillips stayed with the company for ten more years, holding the position of "Chairman of the Board." He died in 1950 at the age of 76. He is buried just outside of Bartlesville, Oklahoma.

Multiple Choice: *Select the choice that completes the statement or answers the question.*

1._____ Which of the following best summarizes how Frank Phillips learned of oil in
Indian Territory?
a. He discovered the oil while on a camping trip with his family.
b. An old friend told him of the oil that could be found in the Osage Nation.
c. He stumbled upon some old geology surveys in a library.
d. A Native American who once lived in the territory suggested where oil could be found.

2._____ Which of the following properly identifies the first oil company Frank Phillips
started with his brother?
a. Anchor Oil & Gas Company   c. Phillips & Phillips Oil and Gas
b. Phillips Petroleum   d. Conoco Oil Company

3._____ Which of the following statements is inaccurate about Frank Phillips and
his brother?
a. The first oil well they drilled struck oil.
b. The brothers made more than $100,000 off of the fourth oil well they drilled.
c. Every well the Phillips brothers drilled was successful.
d. At one point, more than 80 wells in a row were successful for the brothers.

4._____ Which of the following events allowed Frank Phillips to experience his
biggest success?
a. The Spanish-American War   c. World War I
b. The economic boom of the 1920s   d. World War II

5._____ Which of the following statements is inaccurate?
a. Frank Phillips headed Phillips Petroleum for 22 years.
b. The year of Frank Phillips' retirement, the company made $24 million in profits.
c. Phillips held the position of "Chairman of the Board" for ten years after he retired.
d. Today, Frank Phillips is buried just outside of Enid, Oklahoma.

Vocabulary: *Match each word with its correct definition. Consider how the word is used in the lesson. This might help you define each term. Use a dictionary to help if necessary.*

a. apprentice   d. gusher
b. bonds   e. consolidate
c. wildcatter

6._____ a certificate of debt issued to raise funds; repayable at a specified future date

7._____ to bring together into a single, unified whole

8._____ a person who works for another in order to learn a trade

9._____ someone who drills for oil in an area not known for producing oil

10._____ a large capacity, free flowing oil well

Name_____

Guided Reading: *Fill in the blanks below to create complete sentences.*

1. By the time Frank Phillips was 24, he owned three _____.

2. Phillips and his younger _____ organized the Anchor Oil & Gas Company.

3. The fourth well was completed on September 16, 1905, and proved to be a _____.

4. As the United States became more involved in the war, oil prices continued to go _____.

5. Frank Phillips headed _____ for 22 years before finally retiring in 1939.

Correct the Statement: *Each of the following sentences is false. Circle the incorrect word and write the word or phrase that makes the statement correct in the answer blank provided.*

6. In 1874, Frank Phillips was born in Nova Scotia, Canada.
   _____

7. Phillips became an apprentice plumber at the age of 14.
   _____.

8. Phillips met an old friend who told him about the oil that could be found in the Cherokee Nation, in Indian Territory. _____.

9. It wasn't until World War II when Phillips experienced his biggest success.
   _____.

10. Frank Phillips died in 1980, at the age of 76. _____.

Summarize: *Answer the following questions in the space provided. Attempt to respond in a complete sentence for each question. Be sure to use correct capitalization and punctuation.*

1. Who did Frank Phillips start his first oil company with?

2. What did Frank Phillips do while working for his father-in-law? (What did he sell?)

3. When was Phillips Petroleum created?

4. Where is Frank Phillips buried?

5. Why did the Phillips family move to Iowa?

6. How did World War I help the Phillips brothers?

Student Response: *Write a paragraph addressing the questions raised below. A thorough response should consist of three to five complete sentences.*

7. Consider what you have learned about Frank Phillips' life. Had he not been successful in the oil business, do you feel he would have been successful in another business? Why or why not? Cite specific textual evidence from the lesson to support your answer if needed.

The Tulsa Race Massacre

A horrible series of events occurred in Tulsa, Oklahoma in 1921. What precipitated these events? What happened in the aftermath?

Between the years of 1910 and 1920, the city of Tulsa was experiencing enormous growth. The population was soaring as people from all over the country made their way to Tulsa to find work in the blossoming oil industry. As Tulsa grew, Greenwood grew as well.

Greenwood was the African American district, just north of Tulsa. By 1921, Greenwood had a population of more than 15,000 and a host of successful businesses including doctors, lawyers, movie theaters, hotels, and restaurants. Its business district was so successful that Greenwood had become known throughout the nation as "The Black Wall Street". Greenwood had become the wealthiest African American community in the nation.

Words to watch for:
precipitated   apprehended
exaggerated   altercation

Many poor whites living in Tulsa became jealous of the success Greenwood was experiencing. Young men had returned from fighting in World War I and were unable to find work in Tulsa. This mounting frustration greatly contributed to the events that would occur on May 31st and June 1st of 1921.

On May 30th, 1921, a nineteen-year-old African American shoe shiner, Dick Rowland, entered an elevator in the Drexel Building. The elevator operator was a seventeen-year-old white female named Sarah Page. It is unclear what happened, but experts speculate that Dick Rowland lost his balance and reached out to stabilize himself. Miss Page believed she was being assaulted and screamed, which caused Mr. Rowland to run away in fear. Rowland was apprehended by the police and charged with assault.

This incident was reported by the *Tulsa Tribune* in an exaggerated and sensational fashion. In turn, a group of angry white citizens arrived at the courthouse that evening with the intentions of hanging Dick Rowland. Likewise, a large group of blacks arrived at the courthouse with the purpose of protecting Rowland. Tensions were high between the two groups and a scuffle broke out. During the altercation, shots were fired. Suddenly, the entire city erupted into a sea of violence.

The white mob crossed the railroad tracks into Greenwood and began leveling the community. Firebombs were thrown at businesses and homes were burned to the ground, sometimes with families still trapped inside. Many people were shot as they attempted to run away, while others were dragged to death behind vehicles.

Black citizens did not intend to stand idly by while their homes were destroyed and neighbors were killed, so they fought back. Some, who had recently returned from fighting in Europe, began digging trenches and fortifying positions. Greenwood virtually became a warzone.

By the morning of June 1st, Greenwood had been turned into a smoking pile of rubble. The mayor of Tulsa had appealed to the Oklahoma governor to send the National Guard. However, the National Guard did not arrive until late on the morning of June 1st. By this time, most of the fighting had died down. Black rioters were rounded up by the thousands and taken to detention centers.

The official death toll was 39. However, many bodies were hidden or disposed of before they could be counted. Historians estimate that the actual number of dead could be as high as 300. More than 800 were wounded. Thirty-five city blocks were destroyed by fire. This included 191 businesses, a junior high, several churches, and a hospital. More than 10,000 Greenwood residents were left homeless.

Dick Rowland was never charged with a crime. Sarah Page dropped the charges against him, and Rowland was escorted from Tulsa shortly after the incident and never returned to the city.

Following the Tulsa Race Massacre, there was a concentrated effort to omit the incident from state and local history. Newspaper articles about the event were destroyed and it was rarely mentioned in state history textbooks. Many residents of the state grew up without knowing the violence had ever occurred. Finally, in 1996, the state created a commission to study the incident and create a historical account so that the memory of the events could be preserved.

The city of Greenwood never recovered completely. It took more than ten years to rebuild the area. Today, this region is known as North Tulsa.

Multiple Choice: *Select the choice that completes the statement or answers the question.*

1._____ Which of the following best describes Greenwood?
a. Greenwood was a slum in Tulsa where African Americans were forced to live.
b. Greenwood was an all-African American college in eastern Oklahoma.
c. Greenwood was an exclusive white community on the south side of Tulsa.
d. Greenwood was a wealthy African American district just north of Tulsa.

2._____ Which of the following contributed to the events which occurred in Greenwood and Tulsa on May 31st and June 1st of 1921?
a. Young men were frustrated because they could not find work after returning from the war.
b. African Americans were taunting poor whites and teasing them about not being able to find a job.
c. The citizens of Tulsa had forced African Americans to live in slums, which were becoming dangerously overcrowded.
d. An outspoken critic of segregation began giving speeches and stirring the citizens of Greenwood into action.

3._____ Which of the following best summarizes the incident that initiated the violence that occurred in Tulsa and Greenwood in 1921?
a. A young African American male was charged with assault after an unknown incident occurred in an elevator between him and a young white woman.
b. Two rival gangs attacked each other over an incident that had occurred several weeks before. The tension between the two groups had been escalating for days.
c. An African American male was accidentally shot by a white police officer who was attempting to shoot a fleeing suspect.
d. A white female was attacked by an African American female as the two women were both attempting to board the same bus.

4._____ Which of the following best describes Greenwood after the event occurred?
a. Many businesses, churches, a school, and a hospital had been destroyed by fire and more than 10,000 people had been left homeless.
b. The damage was primarily confined to regions of the city where no one lived.
c. There was extensive damage to residential areas in Tulsa, but Greenwood survived the event with very little damage.
d. Greenwood suffered very little damage to homes, but many businesses were destroyed. The people of Greenwood rebuilt over the next year.

5._____ Which of the following statements is inaccurate of the Tulsa Race Massacre?
a. Dick Rowland was never charged with a crime.
b. Following the incident, there was a concentrated effort to omit the event from state and local history.
c. In 1996, the state created a commission to study the incident and create a historical account of the event.
d. The city of Greenwood recovered from the event very quickly.

Vocabulary: *Match each word with its correct definition. Consider how the word is used in the lesson. This might help you define each term. Use a dictionary to help if necessary.*

a. precipitate   d. altercation
b. apprehend   e. omit
c. exaggerate

1._____ to hasten the occurrence of; bring about prematurely

2._____ a heated or angry dispute

3._____ to magnify beyond the limits of truth

4._____ to leave out; fail to mention

5._____ to take into custody; detain

Guided Reading: *Fill in the blanks below to create complete sentences.*

6. By 1921, Greenwood had a population of more than _____ and a host of successful businesses.

7. Many poor whites living in Tulsa became _____ of the success Greenwood was experiencing.

8. The incident was reported on by the _____ in an exaggerated and sensational fashion.

9. The white mob crossed the railroad tracks into _____ and began leveling the community.

10. Black citizens did not intend to stand idly by while their homes were _____ and neighbors were killed.

11. The mayor of Tulsa had appealed to the Oklahoma governor to send the _____.

12. Historians estimate that the actual number of dead could be as high as _____.

13. Dick Rowland was escorted from _____ shortly after the incident and never returned to the city.

14. Newspaper _____ about the event were destroyed, and it was rarely mentioned in state history textbooks.

15. Many residents of the state grew up without knowing the _____ had ever occurred.

Summarize: *Answer the following questions in the space provided. Attempt to respond in a complete sentence for each question. Be sure to use correct capitalization and punctuation!*

1. Who was the young African American shoe shiner who became involved in the incident which eventually led to the Tulsa Race Massacre?

2. What did Greenwood become known as throughout the nation?

3. When did the Tulsa Race Massacre occur?

4. Where was Greenwood located?

5. Why were many poor whites jealous of Greenwood?

6. How were the events surrounding the massacre covered up?

Student Response: *Write a paragraph addressing the questions raised below. A thorough response should consist of three to five complete sentences.*

7. Why do you suppose historians are nearly certain that Dick Rowland did not actually assault the woman that he was arrested for assaulting?

There were many African-American communities throughout Oklahoma in the 1910s and 20s. Utilize a map of Oklahoma and internet resources to locate the following towns.

Cities and towns should be labeled with a •

Boley	Brooksville	Clearview	Langston
Red Bird	Taft	Tullahassee	Vernon

Political Corruption in Oklahoma

The 1920s saw political upheaval in the state of Oklahoma and two governors impeached. What were the issues? Which governors were involved?

Jack Walton experienced a meteoric rise to success after he moved to Oklahoma. In 1917, he was elected as the Commissioner of Public Works, and, not long after that, he became the mayor of Oklahoma City. From that position, he became the 5th governor of Oklahoma in 1923.

Governor Walton became known as "Iron" Jack Walton because he attempted to pursue the Ku Klux Klan, an organization which controlled and manipulated Oklahoma politics, just as they did in many other states. The Klan had so much influence behind the scenes that many referred to them as "the Invisible Empire".

The KKK had a strong presence in Oklahoma and Klan activities were very common in small towns. Some towns even became known as "sundown towns". This meant that African Americans were not safe in these communities after dark.

Governor Walton attempted to face this issue. In an effort to battle the Klan, he sent out the National Guard and declared martial law in several counties. He also suspended habeas corpus, which meant Klan members could be arrested without reason (even if they had committed no known crime). The state legislature believed that he was violating the state constitution, so they prepared to launch an investigation into his actions. As a result, "Iron Jack" placed the entire state under martial law. He became convinced that it was his enemies within the Klan that was orchestrating the investigation.

On October 17th, 1923, the legislature convened in a special session. This was highly unorthodox and possibly illegal, since the governor was the only one legally allowed to call a special session of the legislature. However, they convened without his approval and brought 22 impeachment charges against Walton. These charges included the illegal collection of campaign funds, suspension of habeas corpus, and many other charges. He was convicted by the senate and officially removed from office on November 23rd, 1923. His governorship only lasted ten months, making it one of the shortest in state history.

> *Words to watch for:*
>
> *martial law   unorthodox*
>
> *patronage   impeachment*

Just four years later, Governor Henry Johnston faced several problems of his own. One of the major issues of his administration was patronage. This was a common practice at the time. Governors would appoint those who had financially supported them during the campaign to lucrative and powerful positions. Many felt that Johnston was abusing his power by appointing people who were unqualified for the positions they held.

Governor Johnston had also given a considerable amount of authority to his personal secretary, Mrs. O. O. Hammonds. Mrs. Hammonds controlled the governor's office with a firm grip. No one was admitted to see the governor without her approval. It was also revealed that Mrs. Hammonds may have even been making executive decisions for the governor.

In the wake of these scandals, the state legislature attempted to impeach Governor Johnston. Johnston called out the National Guard and prevented the legislators from entering the state capitol building. The legislature met anyways, in the lobby of the Huckins Hotel in downtown Oklahoma City. Charges were brought against the governor, but they were dismissed by the senate.

In 1928, Governor Johnston chose to endorse Alfred Smith for president. Smith was Catholic and, as a result, was not popular with the Ku Klux Klan. Once again, the Klan manipulated the state legislature in an effort to remove Johnston from office. A second round of impeachment charges was leveled against the governor. The Oklahoma State House of Representatives filed thirteen charges against Johnston. The senate chose to convict him of only one charge, general incompetence. He was officially removed from office on March 20, 1929.

Multiple Choice: *Select the choice that completes the statement or answers the question.*

1._____ Which of the following best explains why Jack Walton became known as "Iron Jack"?
a. Walton was a dedicated railroad worker who laid railroad tracks most of his life.
b. Walton favored the iron industry over the coal industry in several suspicious negotiations.
c. Walton attempted to pursue the Ku Klux Klan and diminish the power they had in the state.
d. Walton frequently carried an iron hammer during campaign speeches, claiming he would "hammer out the injustices".

2._____ Which of the following actions did the state legislature feel was in violation of the state constitution?
a. Governor Walton had called out the National Guard.
b. Governor Walton had declared martial law.
c. Governor Walton had called a special session of the state legislature.
d. Governor Walton had suspended habeas corpus.

3._____ Which of the following was unusual about the special session of the legislature which convened in 1923?
a. This was the first time a governor had ever been impeached in the United States.
b. The legislature met without permission from the governor.
c. This was the last time the legislature has ever met in a special session.
d. The legislature convened in the middle of the night, so that no one would notice.

4._____ Which of the following best summarizes the scandals surrounding Governor Henry Johnston?
a. Many felt he was abusing his power of appointment and giving too much authority to his personal secretary.
b. Many felt that he was taking bribes from certain organizations.
c. It was proven that he was illegally accepting campaign contributions from those living outside of the state.
d. He was caught using state finances to take personal vacations to foreign countries.

5._____ Which of the following best explains why Henry Johnston was probably removed from office?
a. He was found taking bribes from certain businesses.
b. He decided to support a Catholic for president.
c. He threatened to secede from the Union.
d. He attempted to flee the country with large amounts of the state's money.

Vocabulary: *Match each word with its correct definition. Consider how the word is used in the lesson. This might help you define each term. Use a dictionary to help if necessary.*

a. martial law   d. impeachment
b. unorthodox   e. incompetence
c. patronage

6._____ lack of ability; not qualified for a job

7._____ law established and maintained by the military in absence of civilian law

8._____ not conforming to rules or traditions

9._____ the presentation of formal charges against a public official

10._____ the distribution of jobs and favors on a political basis

Name_____

Guided Reading: *Fill in the blanks below to create complete sentences.*

1. Jack Walton became the 5th _____ of Oklahoma in 1923.

2. The KKK had a strong presence in Oklahoma, and _____ activities were very common in small towns.

3. In an effort to battle the Klan, Walton sent out the National Guard and declared _____ in several counties.

4. He also suspended _____, which meant Klan members could be arrested without reason.

5. Governor Walton became convinced that it was his _____ within the Klan that was orchestrating the investigation.

6. The legislature convened without Walton's approval and brought 22 _____ charges against Walton.

7. Governors would appoint those who had _____ supported them during the campaign to lucrative and powerful positions.

8. It was revealed that Mrs. Hammonds may have even been making _____ for Governor Johnston.

9. Johnston called out the National Guard and prevented the legislators from entering the state _____.

10. The Klan _____ the state legislature in an effort to remove Johnston from office.

Summarize: *Answer the following questions in the space provided. Attempt to respond in a complete sentence for each question. Be sure to use correct capitalization and punctuation!*

1. Who was Governor Johnston accused of giving too much authority to?

2. What was the Ku Klux Klan known as by many people?

3. When was Jack Walton officially removed from office?

4. Where did the state legislature meet after being prevented from entering the state capitol building?

5. Why were sundown towns known by this title?

6. How did Governor Johnston's support of Alfred Smith cause him to be impeached and removed from office?

Student Response: *Write a paragraph addressing the questions raised below. A thorough response should consist of three to five complete sentences.*

7. Are you surprised that there was ever a time when the Ku Klux Klan had so much influence over a state's politics? Do you suppose that there are those in politics today who have too much power and influence behind the scenes? Explain your answer as thoroughly as possible.

The 1910s and 20s was an interesting time in Oklahoma. Utilize a map of Oklahoma and internet resources to help you locate and label the following places mentioned in this unit.

Cities and towns should be labeled with a • Rivers should be drawn in using blue and labeled.

Prague	Ada	South Canadian River	Bartlesville
Tulsa	Osage Nation	Greenwood (North Tulsa)	Oklahoma City

Unit Two:
The Dust Bowl

The Dust Bowl

The Dust Bowl was a severe period of drought and dust storms throughout the 1930s. Why did the Dust Bowl happen? How severe was the damage?

The earliest explorers to the Great Plains region of North America determined that the area was unsuitable for agriculture. The territory even became known as "The Great American Desert" because the lack of trees and water made the region relatively unattractive for settlement. However, in the decades following the Civil War, farmers began to settle the region and cultivate the fields under the long-held, but mistaken, belief that "rain will follow the plow."

> *Words to watch for:*
> *agriculture   cultivate*
> *erosion   conservation*

In the first three decades of the 1900s, there were significant and continuous advances in farming technology, including better tractors, mechanized plowing, combines, and more. From 1900 to 1920, the amount of farmland in the plains region doubled, and from 1925 to 1930, the amount of cultivated land tripled!

However, farmers of the era used practices which deprived the soil of its nutrients and increased the possibility of erosion. The heavy plowing had eliminated the natural grasses of the prairie that held the soil in place and maintained moisture.

Then, in 1930, a severe drought struck the Great Plains region, which lasted nearly the entire decade. The regions affected most by this drought were the panhandles of Texas and Oklahoma, western Kansas, and large portions of Colorado and New Mexico. The more than one million acres that was affected became collectively known as "The Dust Bowl".

As the drought grew worse, the topsoil turned to dust and blew away. The blowing dust generated enormous dust storms that reached as far east as Washington D.C.! The dust storms became known as "black blizzards".

During the decade of the 1930s, the Dust Bowl region received anywhere from 15-25% less precipitation than normal. For a region that only sees about twenty inches of rain a year, this means that some areas were receiving as little as fifteen inches of rain in one year (in some years, even less than that!).

As the decade wore on, and the severity of the Dust Bowl increased, efforts were made to correct the conditions. The Civilian Conservation Corps planted more than 200 million trees from Texas to Canada in an attempt to block the wind and hold the soil in place.

Farmers were also instructed in soil conservation techniques such as crop rotation, contour plowing, and terracing. In some cases, the government even paid farmers a dollar an acre to practice one of these conservation techniques. By the end of the 1930s, they had succeeded in reducing the amount of blowing dust by 65%.

By the time the rainfall returned to normal levels, nearly 75% of the topsoil had been blown away in some areas. It would be years before the region recovered completely.

Multiple Choice: *Select the choice that completes the statement or answers the question.*

1._____ Which of the following best describes why the earliest explorers referred to the Great Plains as "the Great American Desert"?
a. The region was covered with sand dunes and the only vegetation was cactus.
b. The region had few trees and was deemed to be unsuitable for agriculture.
c. The region was easily the finest agricultural land ever found.
d. The region had a large number of lizards and other desert dwelling animals.

2._____ Why did farmers begin settling the Great Plains, even though they knew there was little water?
a. There was no other farmland left in the country.
b. Most of the farmers had been forced off their land.
c. New waterless farming techniques had been invented.
d. The farmers believed that rain would follow the plow.

3._____ Why was the soil no longer being held in place?
a. Heavy plowing had eliminated the natural grasses.
b. An excessive number of cattle were trampling the soil.
c. The native grasses had died because of too many pesticides.
d. The soil was being dug up and sold for its high nutrient content.

4._____ The region affected by the drought of the 1930s became known by which of the following names?
a. The Great American Desert   c. The Dust Bowl
b. The Black Blizzard   d. The Little Sahara

5._____ Which of the following methods is not mentioned as a conservation technique used to combat the drought?
a. contour plowing   c. crop rotation
b. digging water wells   d. terracing

Guided Reading: *Fill in the blanks below to create complete sentences.*

1. The Great Plains region of North America became known as the Great American
_____.

2. The lack of trees and _____ made the region relatively
unattractive for settlement.

3. In the early 1900s, there were significant advances in farming technology, including
better tractors, _____ plowing, and combines.

4. Farmers of the era used practices which deprived the soil of its nutrients and
increased the possibility of _____.

5. The regions affected most by drought were the panhandles of Texas and
_____, western Kansas, and parts of Colorado and New Mexico.

6. The dust storms became known as "_____".

7. During the decade of the 1930s, the Dust Bowl region received anywhere from 15-25%
less _____ than normal.

8. The Civilian Conservation Corps planted more than 200 million _____
from Texas to Canada.

9. In some cases, the government even paid farmers a dollar an acre to practice one of
these _____ techniques.

10. By the time the rainfall returned to normal levels, nearly _____ of
the topsoil had been blown away in some regions.

Vocabulary: *Match each word with its correct definition. Consider how the word is used in the lesson.
This might help you define each term. Use a dictionary to help if necessary.*

a. agriculture   d. precipitation
b. cultivate   e. conservation
c. erosion

11._____ rain, snow, sleet, etc. formed by condensation of water vapor in
the atmosphere

12._____ to work land and prepare it for raising crops

13._____ the careful management of natural resources to prevent depletion

14._____ the science or occupation of raising crops and livestock

15._____ the process by which the surface of the earth is worn away by
water and wind

©Reading Through History

Summarize: *Answer the following questions in the space provided. Attempt to respond in a complete sentence for each question. Be sure to use correct capitalization and punctuation!*

1. Who planted more than 200 million trees in an effort to block the wind?

2. What allowed more farmland to be cultivated in the early 1900s?

3. When did the Great Plains experience a severe drought?

4. Where did the blowing dust from the dust storms land? (What city did it reach?)

5. Why did the government pay farmers a dollar an acre?

6. How had the natural grasses of the prairie been eliminated?

Student Response: *Write a paragraph addressing the questions raised below. A thorough response should consist of three to five complete sentences.*

7. The lesson mentions several forms of soil conservation, including contour plowing, terracing, and crop rotation. Use an outside source such as the internet or other resource to research one of these conservation methods. Write a brief description of the process in the space provided.

In the 1930s, Oklahoma and many other states were ravaged by the Dust Bowl. Utilize a map of the United States and internet resources to locate the following places mentioned in this unit, as well as other locations associated with the Dust Bowl. Suggested search terms might include "Dust Bowl region" or "Dust Bowl".

Cities and towns should be labeled with a •

| Texas | Oklahoma | Kansas | Colorado |
| New Mexico | Dust Bowl Region | Nebraska | Dalhart, TX |

Shade each labeled state a different color. Circle the Dust Bowl region.

Black Blizzards

During the 1930s, dust storms ravaged the Great Plains region. The worst of these became known as Black Sunday. When did Black Sunday happen? Just how bad was it?

In the early part of the 20th Century, over-farming, poor soil conservation techniques, and excessive livestock grazing had created a dangerous situation. The topsoil of the Great Plains region had been stripped of its nutrients, as well as the natural vegetation that had once held the soil in place.

Then, 1930 saw the first year of what would eventually be an eleven year drought, in which precipitation (in the form of rainfall, snowfall, and other forms of moisture) was just a fraction of the normal levels.

These factors combined to dehydrate the soil and turn it into a fine, powdery dust. The wind picked up large amounts of this dust and generated massive dust storms which swept across the plains. The storms could reach more than 10,000 feet in height and produce winds from 50 to 80 miles per hour. The storms came to be known as "black blizzards".

The dust storms began in the early 1930s and continued to progress in severity and in number as the decade wore on. In 1932, there were at least fourteen major dust storms, by 1935 there were more than forty, and 1937 saw more than seventy. Historical records of the era were not kept accurately, and some speculate that there may have been more than one hundred dust storms in one year.

Words to watch for:
ravaged   nutrients
speculate   irreparable

The worst of these dust storms occurred on April 14, 1935. The storm blew away an estimated 300 million tons of topsoil in just a few days. The sky became so filled with dirt, that the sun could not be seen. Some witnesses described the event as "a wall of dirt that the eyes could not penetrate". This storm became known as "Black Sunday".

The dust storms affected more than just the Great Plains region. Eastern cities such as Chicago, New York City, Boston, and Washington DC also experienced these massive storms. The skies became so dark that street lights were needed during the day time, and there are even reports that the snow was red in Boston (because the snow was mixing with the soil from a dust storm). Even sailors in the Atlantic Ocean report finding as much as a quarter-inch of dust on the decks of their ships from these massive storms.

Citizens across the nation lived in fear of when the next dust storm would come. As the events became much more commonplace, many learned to recognize the origin of the dust storm by the color of its dirt. Brown dust storms were from Kansas or Nebraska, gray from Texas, and red dust storms were from Oklahoma.

By the late 1930s, the dust storms began to reduce in number. Increased use of soil conservation methods, as well as much needed rainfall, helped to bring the dust storms to an end. However, the damage that had been done was irreparable. Scientists estimate that roughly 30 billion tons of the most nutrient-rich topsoil in the world had simply blown away.

Multiple Choice: *Select the choice that completes the statement or answers the question.*

1._____ Which of the following is not mentioned as one of the causes of the topsoil being stripped of its nutrients in the early part of the 20th Century?
a. over-farming
c. poor soil conservation techniques
b. excessive irrigation
d. excessive livestock grazing

2._____ Which of the following best summarizes the description of a dust storm?
a. Storms reaching more than 50,000 feet and producing winds more than 100 mph.
b. Storms reaching more than 1,000 feet and producing winds from 15 to 20 mph.
c. Storms reaching more than 10,000 feet and producing winds from 50 to 80 mph.
d. Storms reaching more than 100,000 feet and producing winds more than 100 mph.

3._____ The dust storm which occurred on April 14, 1935 came to be known by what name?
a. Black Tuesday
c. Black Monday
b. Black Friday
d. Black Sunday

4._____ Which of the following statements is false?
a. The skies became so dark in cities that street lights were needed during the day.
b. Many people were confused by the darkness and mistakenly believed it was night.
c. There are reports of red snow in Boston because it had mixed with dirt.
d. Sailors in the Atlantic Ocean reported that there was a quarter-inch of dust on the decks of their ships.

5._____ Which of the following does not correctly match a state with the color of its soil/dust storms?
a. yellow dust storms were from Nebraska
b. brown dust storms were from Kansas
c. gray dust storms were from Texas
d. red dust storms were from Oklahoma

Guided Reading: *Fill in the blanks below to create complete sentences.*

1. The topsoil of the Great Plains region had been stripped of its nutrients as well as the natural _____ that had once held the soil in place.

2. 1930 saw the first year of what would eventually be an eleven year _____.

3. These factors combined to dehydrate the soil and turn it into a fine, powdery _____.

4. In 1937, there were more than _____ dust storms.

5. On April 14, 1935, a dust storm blew away an estimated _____ tons of topsoil.

6. The sky became so filled with dirt, that the _____ could not be seen.

7. Eastern cities such as Chicago, _____, Boston, and Washington DC also experienced these massive storms.

8. Citizens lived in fear of the dust storms, but the storms also became much more _____.

9. By the late 1930s, the dust storms began to _____ in number.

10. Increased use of soil conservation methods, as well as much needed _____, helped to bring the dust storms to an end.

Vocabulary: *Match each word with its correct definition. Consider how the word is used in the lesson. This might help you define each term. Use a dictionary to help if necessary.*

a. ravage
b. nutrients
c. dehydrate

d. speculate
e. irreparable

11._____ to cause severe damage to

12._____ to lose water; to cause to lose water

13._____ unable to be fixed; beyond repair

14._____ to make a guess without knowing the complete facts

15._____ any substance that nourishes an organism or plant

Summarize: *Answer the following questions in the space provided. Attempt to respond in a complete sentence for each question. Be sure to use correct capitalization and punctuation!*

1. Who reported finding dust on the decks of their ships?

2. What nickname was given to the dust storms?

3. When did "Black Sunday" occur?

4. Which states did the dust storms come from?

5. Why did the dust storms reduce in number in the late 1930s?

6. How many tons of topsoil got blown away (in all)?

Student Response: *Write a paragraph addressing the questions raised below. A thorough response should consist of three to five complete sentences.*

7. Imagine being caught in a severe dust storm similar to the one that occurred on Black Sunday. Write a brief narrative describing the sights, sounds, tastes, etc. that you experience. Use as much descriptive language as possible. Use additional paper if necessary.

Dust Pneumonia & Dust Storm Preparations

One of the worst health conditions from the Dust Bowl era was dust pneumonia. What was dust pneumonia? What methods did Dust Bowl residents use to try and combat the encroaching dust?

During the 1930s, when the Great Plains region was being plagued by a drought and ravaged by dust storms, a new physical ailment emerged. It was known as dust pneumonia, and it was caused by breathing in dust from the air. Dirt would fill the lungs and cause coughing, tightness of the chest, labored breathing, and shortness of breath.

Children and the elderly were affected the most, with deaths being common. Many were hospitalized because of this condition, but it is difficult to tell exact numbers because medical records from the era were either not kept, or not well preserved.

Those who lived in the Dust Bowl tried many methods to combat the dust and keep themselves healthy. Parents would have their children sleep with sheets over their beds, like a tent, to reduce the amount of dust they inhaled during their sleep. Dust masks and wet cloths over the mouth were other methods that some used to try and prevent dust inhalation. Additionally, goggles were sometimes worn to keep blowing dust out of the eyes.

Housewives made many efforts to keep the dirt and dust out of the home. Sometimes these activities were as simple as constantly sweeping the floors. Other methods were more significant, such as tacking bed sheets in front of doors and windows, wetting them down in an effort to keep out as much dust as possible. They also used strips of cloth, soaked in a paste made of flour and water, to insulate the outer edges of windows, trying to seal them shut.

While humans could take these measures, animals were not so lucky. Cattle and other livestock had little shelter and nowhere to run from the dust storms. Many families were forced to watch helplessly as their animals died from dust inhalation. No livestock meant no meat, eggs, milk, or other dairy products, which only added more hardship to their lives.

Words to watch for:

pneumonia encroaching

inhalation insulation

The dust was everywhere. Residents of the Dust Bowl region lived in it, breathed it, slept in it, and even ate it (many Dust Bowl survivors testify that they could feel the gritty dirt in their food). There was no escaping it. The measures mentioned above helped reduce the dust some, but it was a constant presence in their lives.

Multiple Choice: *Select the choice that completes the statement or answers the question.*

1._____ Which of the following caused dust pneumonia?
a. eating dust particles in food
b. dust infecting the eyes
c. breathing in large amounts of dust
d. there was no known cause for it

2._____ Which of the following is *not* mentioned as a method of preventing exposure
        to dust?
a. sleeping with sheets over the bed   c. wet cloths over the mouth
b. frequent baths to wash the dust off   d. goggles to keep dust out of the eyes

3._____ Which of the following is not an accurate statement?
a. Bed sheets were placed in front of doors and windows to help keep dust out.
b. Strips of cloth soaked in flour and water were used to seal windows shut.
c. Housewives living in the Dust Bowl swept their floors frequently.
d. New electronic humidifiers were used to help add moisture to homes.

4._____ What is the primary reason the loss of livestock added to the hardship in
        people's lives?
a. Many animals were beloved pets, and their loss was heartbreaking.
b. There was a heavy tax charged for every animal that was lost.
c. The loss of these animals meant no meat, eggs, or dairy products.
d. Many farmers still depended on livestock to pull their plows.

5._____ Which of the following statements is true?
a. Many Dust Bowl survivors say they could feel the gritty dirt in their food.
b. There were very few people who lived through the Dust Bowl.
c. Dust pneumonia was almost always fatal.
d. Children and the elderly were rarely inflicted with dust pneumonia.

©Reading Through History

Guided Reading: *Fill in the blanks below to create complete sentences.*

1. A new physical ailment known as dust _____ was caused by breathing in large amounts of dust.

2. Dirt would fill the lungs, and cause _____, tightness of the chest, heavy breathing, and shortness of breath.

3. It is difficult to tell how many people were inflicted with dust pneumonia because _____ records from the era were not well preserved.

4. Parents would have their children sleep with sheets over their beds to reduce the amount of dust they _____ during their sleep.

5. _____ were sometimes worn to keep blowing dust out of the eyes.

6. Housewives would tack _____ in front of doors and windows, wetting them down in an effort to keep out as much dust as possible.

7. They also used strips of cloth, soaked in a paste made of _____ and water, to insulate the outer edges of windows.

8. Cattle and other livestock had little _____ from the dust storms.

9. Many families were forced to watch helplessly as their _____ died from dust inhalation.

10. For those living in the Dust Bowl, _____ was a constant presence in their lives.

Vocabulary: *Match each word with its correct definition. Consider how the word is used in the lesson. This might help you define each term. Use a dictionary to help if necessary.*

a. pneumonia
b. encroach
c. ailment

d. inhalation
e. insulation

11._____ inflammation of the lungs, characterized by coughing and difficulty breathing

12._____ the act of breathing in

13._____ a physical disorder or illness

14._____ to intrude or advance beyond the usual limits

15._____ material used to protect something from heat, cold, or wind

Summarize: *Answer the following questions in the space provided. Attempt to respond in a complete sentence for each question. Be sure to use correct capitalization and punctuation.*

1. Who was the most affected by dust pneumonia?

2. What were the symptoms of dust pneumonia?

3. When was the Great Plains plagued by drought?

4. Where could Dust Bowl residents find an escape from the dust?

5. Why did parents put sheets over their children's beds?

6. How were wet bed sheets used during the Dust Bowl?

Student Response: *Write a paragraph addressing the questions raised below. A thorough response should consist of three to five complete sentences.*

7. What do you think the most difficult part about living during the Dust Bowl would have been? Explain your answer.

Rabbits, Grasshoppers & Other Problems

*The dirt and dust storms of the Dust Bowl era were just the beginning of farmers'
problems in the 1930s. What were some of the other problems they faced?*

As a severe drought ravaged the Great Plains, and the
huge dust storms further altered the ecology of the
region, new waves of pests began sweeping across the
prairie.

The worst of these new varmints were jackrabbits.
Jackrabbits breed at an amazing rate, producing as
many as eight young a month. Normally, jackrabbit
populations are kept at normal levels because of their
natural predators such as coyotes. However, during
the Dust Bowl, those predators had either died, or
moved on to other regions in search of water.

With no natural predators, the jackrabbit population surged to unbelievable levels, and
they became a major pest across the plains as they ate grass and crops. In an effort to
reduce the jackrabbit population, residents across the Dust Bowl region held rabbit
drives, rounding up the animals and disposing of them. In one rabbit drive, which
took place in Kansas, they captured more than 35,000 rabbits in one afternoon.

Grasshoppers became another nightmare during the Dust Bowl. Just like the
jackrabbits, the grasshopper's natural predators (birds and rodents) had moved on in
search of water. Grasshoppers travelled in swarms across the land, with as many as
23,000 insects per acre. They devoured virtually everything in their path.

Many efforts were utilized to try and curtail the plague of grasshoppers. The National
Guard burned infested fields and even crushed the insects with tractors. The Civilian
Conservation Corps spread large amounts of insecticide which was made from arsenic,
molasses, and bran.

Inside houses, other types of insects were a danger as well. Poisonous centipedes and
deadly spiders infiltrated homes in search of shade or water. There are some reports of
women filling entire buckets full of these types of pests.

Words to watch for:
ecology   curtail
devoured   infested

Static electricity created a different type of danger. Friction
caused by blowing dust particles rubbing together, and
against metal objects, created large amounts of static
electricity. This electricity was powerful enough to kill crops
and even knock a person unconscious. Many Dust Bowl
survivors remember seeing blue arcs of static electricity at
night, coming from windmills and barbed wire fences.

These were just a few of the additional dangers that many people endured during the
Dust Bowl.

Multiple Choice: *Select the choice that completes the statement or answers the question.*

1._____ Why did the jackrabbit population surge during the Dust Bowl?
a.   Most of the jackrabbit's predators had either died or moved to other areas.
b.   Jackrabbits are one of the few animals that don't need water to survive.
c.   A new law had been passed which outlawed the hunting of jackrabbits.
d.   Jackrabbits experienced a short-lived popularity as a household pet.

2._____ Which of the following best describes how the people living in the Dust Bowl
            dealt with the problem of rabbits?
a.   They built fences to keep the rabbits out.
b.   They adopted as many of them as they could as pets.
c.   They sprayed poisons to kill the rabbits.
d.   They had rabbit drives and rounded the animals up.

3._____ Why were grasshoppers a pest during the Dust Bowl era?
a.   The grasshoppers bite became infected and itched severely.
b.   Grasshoppers were poisonous and could kill a victim in seconds.
c.   The grasshoppers devoured everything in their path.
d.   Grasshoppers created a lot of noise, and no one could sleep.

4._____ Which of the following is not mentioned as a method for killing
            grasshoppers?
a. poisoning their food supply   c. burning infested fields
b. crushing with tractors   d. spraying pesticides

5._____ Which of the following reasons accurately describes why static electricity
            could be dangerous?
a.   Static electricity could accidentally start machinery which could injure people.
b.   Static electricity could easily kill someone who stepped outside.
c.   Static electricity could kill crops or knock someone unconscious.
d.   Static electricity could cause illnesses, such as dust pneumonia.

Name_____

Guided Reading: *Fill in the blanks below to create complete sentences.*

1. As dust storms altered the ecology of the region, new waves of _____ began sweeping across the prairie.

2. Jackrabbits can produce as many as _____ young a month.

3. During the Dust Bowl, the jackrabbit's natural predators had either died or moved on to other regions in search of _____.

4. With no natural _____, the jackrabbit population surged to unbelievable levels.

5. In one rabbit drive, which took place in Kansas, they captured more than _____ rabbits in one afternoon.

6. Grasshoppers moved in _____ across the land, with as many as 23,000 insects per acre.

7. The Civilian Conservation Corps also spread large amounts of insecticide which was made from _____, molasses, and bran.

8. Poisonous _____ and deadly spiders infiltrated homes in search of shade or water.

9. There are some reports of women filling entire _____ full of these types of pests.

10. Many Dust Bowl survivors remember seeing blue _____ of static electricity at night.

Vocabulary: *Match each word with its correct definition. Consider how the word is used in the lesson. This might help you define each term. Use a dictionary to help if necessary.*

a. ecology
b. predator
c. curtail

d. devour
e. infest

11._____ to eat up hungrily

12._____ to live in, or inhabit in dangerously large numbers

13._____ the relation between organisms and their environment

14._____ to cut short; reduce or diminish

15._____ an animal that preys upon another animal

Summarize: *Answer the following questions in the space provided. Attempt to respond in a complete sentence for each question. Be sure to use correct capitalization and punctuation!*

1. Who was utilized to crush grasshoppers with tractors and burn infested fields?

2. What was the insecticide made from?

3. When could people see blue arcs of static electricity?

4. Where did the 35,000 rabbit drive take place?

5. Why did the grasshoppers become a nightmare?

6. How was static electricity created?

Student Response: *Write a paragraph addressing the questions raised below. A thorough response should consist of three to five complete sentences.*

7. This lesson discussed many different pests and problems related to the Dust Bowl. Of these pests, which do you think would be the worst to deal with? Thoroughly explain your answer.

Despite earning the nickname "The Great American Desert", Oklahoma has numerous lakes which are used for recreation and to produce hydroelectric energy. Utilize a map of Oklahoma and internet resources to help you locate and label the following Oklahoma lakes and reservoirs.

Lakes should be drawn in and shaded using blue.

Lake Texoma	Lake Eufala	Grand Lake o' the Cherokees	Kaw Lake
Tenkiller Ferry Lake	Oologah Lake	Robert S. Kerr Reservoir	Broken Bow Lake

Unit Three:
Okies

Okies

As the Dust Bowl made life increasingly difficult for those living in the central plains, many people decided to abandon their homes in search of new opportunities. Who were these people? Where did they go?

Many left the Dust Bowl region in favor of trying to find a job in the city. Others decided to leave the area altogether. Most of those who left had a common destination, California. Writers of the era observed that the highways between Oklahoma and California resembled a parade, with a continuous string of cars heading west. Others compared it to the gold rush of 1849, with millions of migrants moving in search of a fresh start.

In 1934 alone, Oklahoma lost more than 400,000 people. That same year, Kansas lost over 200,000. The plains states as a whole experienced a loss of 2.5 million people. Oklahoma suffered the most in terms of population loss. Other states lost 3% or 4% of their population, but some estimates claim that Oklahoma lost as much as 18% of its total population.

Not all of the Dust Bowl refugees were from Oklahoma, but because so many of them were, the Californians had a nickname for all of them. They called them Okies. Journalist Ben Reddick first used the term "Okie" in his articles after noticing the "OK" abbreviation on many of the migrant license plates.

Most of these Okies were heading to California because they thought they could find jobs picking fruit. After all, California supplied nearly half of the fresh fruit for the entire country. However, there were multiple downsides to this occupation.

First, there were far more workers than were needed. With such a surplus of laborers, employers could pay extremely low wages (there was no minimum wage at that time). Additionally, many jobs only lasted two or three days, at which point the worker needed to move on to the next location in order to find more work. This forced the Okies into a migratory lifestyle, constantly moving on to the next orchard, grove, or vineyard.

> *Words to watch for:*
>
> migrant   refugees
>
> surplus   plight

Given the migrant lifestyle and low pay, the Okies lived a very hard, unpleasant life. They were looked down upon by Californians and many towns refused to permit them entrance. They were forced to live outside of communities in makeshift villages of shacks and other poorly built shelters. These places became known as Little Oklahomas. Because these communities were filthy, with little proper sanitation and no running water, diseases such as typhus and diphtheria became widespread.

To help expose the plight of the Okies, a writer named John Steinbeck wrote a book in 1939 titled *The Grapes of Wrath*. This novel told the story of Tom Joad and his family as they traveled from Oklahoma to California and their hardships once they arrived.

Eventually, the U.S. government attempted to help the Okies living in California. Camps were organized to provide better toilet and bathing facilities as well as community cooking areas and laundry rooms. By 1941, there were 13 of these camps across California with about 45,000 people living in them.

The nickname "Okie" was originally used by Californians as an insult. In *The Grapes of Wrath*, the main character Tom Joad observed, "Okie means you're scum." However, in modern times, many people from Oklahoma have embraced the nickname and use it with pride, just as a Hoosier from Indiana or a Yankee from New England uses those nicknames.

Multiple Choice: *Select the choice that completes the statement or answers the question.*

1._____ Which of the following explanations best describes why many people left the Dust Bowl region?
a. Many went to find work elsewhere because the Dust Bowl had made life too difficult.
b. Many left because the pesticides used to kill insects had made the area unlivable.
c. Many left because the government had instructed them to leave for their own safety.
d. Many went to prospect for gold in California, just as others had in 1849.

2._____ Why were many Oklahomans moving to California?
a. They were attempting to mine for gold, just as others had in 1849.
b. They were going to find jobs picking fruit in orchards and vineyards.
c. They were attempting to make it big in Hollywood, just like other movie stars.
d. They were going to find jobs in the fishing industry.

3._____ Which of the following is not mentioned as a downside to the occupation the Okies were engaged in?
a. Jobs would only last two or three days.
b. Wages were extremely low.
c. The job required skills they did not have.
d. They were forced to live a migratory lifestyle.

4._____ Why were diseases such as typhus and diphtheria common?
a. There was no known cure for either of these diseases at the time.
b. Typhus and diphtheria are spread by mosquitos, a common pest in the camps.
c. A plague of these two diseases was infecting the entire nation at that time.
d. The communities the Okies were forced to live in were filthy and had little sanitation.

5._____ How did the U.S. government assist the Okies?
a. The government provided trucks and buses to help them return to Oklahoma.
b. The government established camps with running water and bathing facilities.
c. The government gave each family a subsidy check which allowed them to buy food.
d. The government gave each family a homestead to start a farm.

Name_____

Guided Reading: *Fill in the blanks below to create complete sentences.*

1. Writers of the era observed that the highways between Oklahoma and California resembled a _____, with a continuous string of cars heading west.

2. Some estimates claim that Oklahoma lost as much as _____ of its total population.

3. Because so many of the refugees came from Oklahoma, the Californians nicknamed them _____.

4. California supplied nearly half of the fresh _____ for the entire country.

5. Okies lived a _____ lifestyle, constantly moving on to the next orchard, grove, or vineyard.

6. Okies were looked down upon by _____ and many towns refused to permit them entrance.

7. Diseases such as typhus and _____ became widespread in the Okie camps.

8. _____ told the story of Tom Joad and his family as they traveled from Oklahoma to California.

9. By 1941, there were 13 camps across California with about _____ people living in them.

10. In modern times, many people from Oklahoma have embraced the nickname "Okie" and use it with _____.

Vocabulary: *Match each word with its correct definition. Consider how the word is used in the lesson. This might help you define each term. Use a dictionary to help if necessary.*

a. migrant
b. refugee
c. surplus

d. sanitation
e. plight

11._____ a condition, state, or situation

12._____ a person who has fled some danger or problem

13._____ the disposal of sewage and solid waste

14._____ greater than the needed amount

15._____ a person who moves from one place to another

Summarize: *Answer the following questions in the space provided. Attempt to respond in a complete sentence for each question. Be sure to use correct capitalization and punctuation!*

1. Who first used the term "Okie" in his writings?

2. What were the villages the Okies lived in known as?

3. When did John Steinbeck write *The Grapes of Wrath*?

4. Where did most of the migrants who left the Dust Bowl region go?

5. Why were employers able to pay such low wages to the migrant workers?

6. How was the term "Okie" originally used by Californians?

Student Response: *Write a paragraph addressing the questions raised below. A thorough response should consist of three to five complete sentences.*

7. Use an outside resource, such as the internet, to research typhus and diphtheria. Use the space below to describe the symptoms of these two diseases.

Route 66 became an important highway during the years of the Dust Bowl. Utilize a map of the United States and internet resources to locate and label the following places along Route 66. Suggested search terms might include "Route 66" or "important cities on Route 66".

Draw in and label the route itself in gray or black. Cities should be labeled with a •

Route 66   Illinois   Oklahoma   California
Chicago   Tulsa   Oklahoma City   Albuquerque

Color each labeled state a different color.

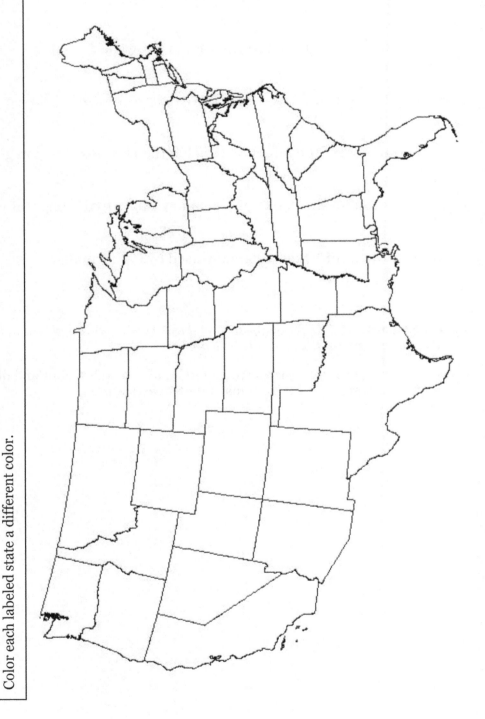

The Grapes of Wrath

In 1939, John Steinbeck wrote a novel which would become one of the most controversial books of all time. It would also become one of the most celebrated works of American literature. What was this novel? Why was it so controversial?

The Grapes of Wrath focuses on the Joad family, poor share-croppers from Oklahoma who have to leave their home because of the Dust Bowl and the other economic hardships associated with the Great Depression. In an effort to change their luck, they set out for California, along with thousands of other Okies.

The book was first published on March 14, 1939. By May, it was at the top of the best sellers list, and by the end of 1939, almost 500,000 copies had been sold. Its price of $2.75 was fairly reasonable at the time, which allowed many people to purchase copies. Even those who had never read a book before were buying it. Book stores were sold out, and there were waiting lists at libraries that were months long.

The book paints an incredibly vivid picture of the hardships endured by the Dust Bowl's migrant workers. It also illustrates how the migrants were treated after arriving in California. When people read it, they were shocked by the poverty and hopelessness presented in the story.

However, not everyone liked what they were reading. There were claims that the book exaggerated the hardships of the Okies. Many declared that it was impossible for such horrible circumstances to exist in the United States of America. Also, citizens of California were displeased with the way Steinbeck portrayed the Californian attitude towards the migrants. The Associated Farmers of California denounced the book as a pack of lies.

Some criticized the novel for other reasons. It emphasized cooperative solutions to economic problems instead of individualistic solutions. Because of these themes, many people felt it was pro-socialist or pro-communist.

Because of the book's controversial nature, it was banned from many libraries across the country. One group in California called for "widespread denouncement against the book before school opens and our boys and girls find such filthy material on the shelves of our public library."

Words to watch for:
share-croppers   controversial
exaggerated   denounced

National radio programs debated the merits of the book, and it was even publicly burned in Buffalo, New York; East St. Louis, Illinois; and in several communities in California. Oklahoma Representative Lyle Boren went as far as denouncing the book in Congress as a vulgar lie. However, much of this uproar died down when Eleanor Roosevelt praised the book and defended Steinbeck.

In 1939, _The Grapes of Wrath_ won the Pulitzer Prize for a Novel, and the popularity of the book has endured to this day. John Steinbeck's novel has been translated into many different languages including French, German, and Japanese.

The Grapes of Wrath remains banned in many school libraries across the nation. However, it is probably the most discussed and debated American novel of the 20th Century and will always be considered one of the classics of American literature.

Multiple Choice: *Select the choice that completes the statement or answers the question.*

1._____ Which of the following best describes why the Joad family has to leave their home in *The Grapes of Wrath*?
a. They are forced off their land by a corrupt landlord.
b. A severe flood has wiped out their crops and they're searching for drier land.
c. They are trying to escape the hardships of the Dust Bowl.
d. A tornado destroyed their home, so they were searching for a new one.

2._____ Which of the following best summarizes why audiences were so interested in *The Grapes of Wrath*?
a. The book told a fascinating story about hobos riding trains.
b. The book was unlike any other that had ever been written before.
c. The book was filled with violence and foul language, which audiences were attracted to.
d. The book helped readers understand the hardships endured by migrant workers in California.

3._____ Which of the following is *not* one of the reasons why *The Grapes of Wrath* was controversial?
a. Some claimed that the book exaggerated the hardships endured by the Okies.
b. Some were angry that it made Oklahomans look too polite.
c. Some were displeased with the way Steinbeck depicted Californians' treatment of the Okies.
d. Some thought the novel was pro-communist because it stressed collective solutions to economic problems.

4._____ Which of the following reasons best describes why the uproar over *The Grapes of Wrath* softened?
a. Eleanor Roosevelt praised the novel and defended John Steinbeck.
b. Another novel came out which was even more controversial.
c. A Representative from the state of Oklahoma praised the book.
d. John Steinbeck issued a public apology and asked for forgiveness.

5._____ Which of the following statements about *The Grapes of Wrath* is an opinion?
a. *The Grapes of Wrath* caused a great deal of controversy.
b. *The Grapes of Wrath* has been translated into many different languages.
c. *The Grapes of Wrath* is a classic work of American literature.
d. *The Grapes of Wrath* won the Pulitzer Prize for a Novel.

Guided Reading: *Fill in the blanks below to create complete sentences.*

1. *The Grapes of Wrath* focuses on the _____ family.

2. In an effort to change their luck, the family sets out for _____, along with thousands of other Okies.

3. *The Grapes of Wrath* cost _____ to purchase, which was a fairly reasonable price for the time.

4. When people read *The Grapes of Wrath*, they were shocked by the poverty and _____ presented in the story.

5. Many claimed that it was impossible for such horrible circumstances to exist in _____.

6. *The Grapes of Wrath* emphasized cooperative solutions to economic problems instead of _____ solutions.

7. Because of the book's controversial nature, it was _____ from libraries all across the country.

8. National radio programs debated the _____ of the book.

9. The popularity of the book has _____ to this day.

10. *The Grapes of Wrath* remains banned in many school _____ across the nation.

Vocabulary: *Match each word with its correct definition. Consider how the word is used in the lesson. This might help you define each term. Use a dictionary to help if necessary.*

a. share-cropper
b. controversial
c. exaggerate

d. denounce
e. vulgar

11._____ to make a formal accusation against; attack

12._____ a farmer who pays a share of the crop as rent

13._____ an issue that there is a strong disagreement over

14._____ indecent or obscene

15._____ to present as larger, or greater than is true

Summarize: *Answer the following questions in the space provided. Attempt to respond in a complete sentence for each question. Be sure to use correct capitalization and punctuation!*

1. Who denounced the book as a pack of lies? (Which organization?)

2. What award did *The Grapes of Wrath* win?

3. When was *The Grapes of Wrath* first published?

4. Where was *The Grapes of Wrath* burned?

5. Why did Californians not like *The Grapes of Wrath*?

6. How is *The Grapes of Wrath* viewed today?

Student Response: *Write a paragraph addressing the questions raised below. A thorough response should consist of three to five complete sentences.*

7. If you had been living in the Dust Bowl region in the 1930s, would you have stayed and toughed it out? Or would you have tried to leave and find better conditions, as the Joad family did? Explain your answer.

Alfalfa Bill Murray

One of the most charismatic and controversial governors of the 1930s was Governor William H. Murray from Oklahoma. What did Murray do to become so well-known? Why did he become controversial?

William H. Murray was born in Toadsuck, Texas on November 21, 1869. The family moved to Montague, Texas after his mother died and his father remarried. At the age of twelve, young Bill decided to leave home. He was eventually adopted by another family who had him attending school in the winter and working on farms during the summer.

As he got older, he worked as a salesman, a teacher, a newspaper reporter, and a lawyer. But, he was first and foremost a farmer. He always liked to tell people that he "believed in the family farm, the values of Thomas Jefferson, and the greatness of the Democratic Party."

In 1898, Murray moved to Tishomingo, which was the capital of the Chickasaw Nation in Indian Territory. He became involved in politics while living in Indian Territory and served as one of the representatives at the Sequoyah Convention. This was a meeting which attempted to create a state out of Indian Territory (the eastern half of present-day Oklahoma).

Murray was also president of the constitutional convention when Oklahoma finally became a state in 1907. He was the state's first Speaker of the House, a member of Congress, and he ran for governor twice and lost, all before 1924. Bill Murray seemed to be a constant figure in Oklahoma politics. In many of his speeches, he frequently referred to a plot of land which he grew alfalfa on. One newspaper referred to him as "Alfalfa Bill" in a column. The nickname stayed with him throughout the remainder of his life.

Then, in 1924, Murray and his wife led a group of American colonists, most of them Oklahomans, to Bolivia. Once they were in Bolivia, they attempted to establish an agrarian colony. The attempt failed miserably, and only five years later, in 1929, they returned to Oklahoma.

Alfalfa Bill had lost all of his money in the effort. So, he borrowed $40 from a bank in Tishomingo and started a campaign for governor. Murray traveled across the state in a worn-out car, stopping at street corners to give speeches. He ate his lunch out of a paper bag while talking about politics with anyone who would listen. He was frequently unshaven and his clothes were dirty. He presented himself as a down to earth common man. He won the 1930 election by more than 100,000 votes, becoming Oklahoma's ninth governor. This was the largest victory of any Oklahoma governor up to that time.

Words to watch for:

charismatic   controversial

agrarian   martial law

During his career as governor, Murray called out the National Guard on 47 occasions and declared martial law 30 times. The most famous of these was the two month incident known as the "Toll Bridge War". In the summer of 1931, Oklahoma National Guardsmen faced off against Texas Rangers over a "free bridge" that had been built across the Red River to replace an older toll bridge. When the governor of Texas, Ross Sterling, sent Rangers to barricade the Texas side of the new bridge (as part of a court injunction), Governor Murray sent National Guardsmen to remove the barricades and keep roads to the bridge open. The Texas injunction against the new bridge was eventually dissolved.

As governor, Murray became one of the early national leaders in the effort to help those hurt by the Great Depression. He used his own salary to feed the poor and collected money from state employees and businessmen to finance relief programs to aid those suffering during the economic crisis.

Alfalfa Bill's popularity even carried him onto the national scene. In 1932, he attempted to become the Democrat nominee for president. He participated in several primary elections, but eventually lost the nomination to Franklin D. Roosevelt.

Multiple Choice: *Select the choice that completes the statement or answers the question.*

1._____ Which of the following best summarizes William H. Murray's early political career?
a. Murray served as an aide to a governor and was then elected lieutenant governor.
b. Murray served as a representative to the Sequoyah Convention and president of the Oklahoma Constitutional Convention.
c. Murray was a complete unknown prior to running for governor, but he still won his first election in a landslide.
d. Murray was appointed to a seat in the U.S. Senate before returning to Oklahoma to run for governor.

2._____ Which of the following best explains why William H. Murray was known as "Alfalfa Bill"?
a. He was frequently spotted chewing on a piece of alfalfa.
b. It was a common nickname for people from Oklahoma.
c. It was a childhood nickname that an old friend had given him.
d. He frequently referred to a plot of land which he grew alfalfa on.

3._____ Which of the following statements is *not* true of William H. Murray?
a. He was the first Speaker of the House in Oklahoma.
b. He led a group of colonists to Bolivia in 1924.
c. He borrowed $40 in order to run for governor.
d. He won the closest governor's election in the history of Oklahoma.

4._____ Which of the following best summarizes the "Toll Bridge War"?
a. Oklahoma and Texas were engaged in a dispute over the use of a free bridge that crossed the Red River.
b. Governor Murray attempted to implement a statewide system requiring tolls to be paid in order to cross all bridges.
c. Governor Murray refused to clear bridges of ice and snow unless a toll was paid by each county.
d. Oklahoma and Kansas were having a disagreement over the building of bridges that passed from one state to the other.

5._____ Which of the following helped make William H. Murray a nationally significant figure?
a. He was very outspoken against President Roosevelt and the US Congress.
b. He had a radio program which was listened to by 30 million people every week.
c. He wrote a weekly newspaper column that was read by millions across the nation.
d. He was one of the early leaders who helped the poor during the Great Depression.

©Reading Through History

Guided Reading: *Fill in the blanks below to create complete sentences.*

1. William H. Murray was born in _____, Texas.

2. Murray worked as a salesman, a teacher, a newspaper reporter, and a lawyer, but he was first and foremost a _____.

3. In 1898, Murray moved to Tishomingo, which was the capital of the Chickasaw Nation in _____.

4. Murray was also president of the constitutional convention when Oklahoma finally became a state in _____.

5. Murray took a group of colonists to Bolivia where they attempted to establish an _____ colony.

6. While campaigning for governor, Murray presented himself as a down to earth _____.

7. Murray called out the _____ on 47 different occasions.

8. Murray also declared martial law _____ times.

9. Murray collected money from state employees and businessmen to finance _____ in the early stages of the Great Depression.

10. In 1932, Alfalfa Bill Murray attempted to become the _____ nominee for president.

Vocabulary: *Match each word with its correct definition. Consider how the word is used in the lesson. This might help you define each term. Use a dictionary to help if necessary.*

a. charismatic
b. controversial
c. agrarian

d. martial law
e. finance

11._____ a subject in which there are strong disagreements of opinion over

12._____ a quality in an individual which makes the person influential, charming, or inspiring; the ability to create great enthusiasm in others

13._____ related to the land or farming

14._____ to supply with money or capital; to pay for

15._____ law imposed by military force

Summarize: *Answer the following questions in the space provided. Attempt to respond in a complete sentence for each question. Be sure to use correct capitalization and punctuation!*

1. Who did the Oklahoma National Guard face off against during the "Toll Bridge War"?

2. What was the Sequoyah Convention?

3. When was William H. Murray elected governor of Oklahoma?

4. Where did Alfalfa Bill Murray go in 1924?

5. Why did William H. Murray have to borrow money to run for governor?

6. Other than collecting money from state employees and businessmen, how did William H. Murray help the poor?

Student Response: *Write a paragraph addressing the questions raised below. A thorough response should consist of three to five complete sentences.*

7. Alfalfa Bill Murray called out the National Guard 47 times and instituted martial law 30 times while he was governor. Do you feel that governors should be able to use military force in that way? Why or Why not? Support your answer.

Will Rogers

One of the most enduring figures of the 1930s was Will Rogers. Who was Will Rogers? What did he become famous for?

Will Rogers was born in 1879 in Indian Territory, near present-day Oologah, Oklahoma. His parents were both part Cherokee. He was the youngest of eight children, but only three of his siblings survived into adulthood.

In 1901, Rogers heard that there was money to be made in Argentina. So, he and a friend headed out in search of their fortunes. When they arrived in Argentina, they discovered that the money they dreamed of was a myth. So, his friend went back to Oklahoma, but Will stayed. From there, he got a job on a boat that was headed for South Africa.

In South Africa, he went to work on a ranch and was eventually hired by Texas Jack's Wild West Show. He appeared in the shows as "The Cherokee Kid" and became famous for performing rope tricks. He toured South Africa with the Wild West Show until he was hired by a circus that took him to Australia and New Zealand.

In 1904, he returned to the United States and started performing vaudeville in New York City. Vaudeville was a form of variety show which usually featured singers, dancers, jugglers, comedians, and other performers. Rogers performed his tricks and told jokes to the audience as he twirled his rope. The sophisticated New York audiences loved Will's country accent. He also had a natural sense of humor that crowds appreciated. Rogers would often open each show by saying, "All I know is what I read in the papers". He would then joke about current events and poke fun at political figures of the era.

By 1916, he was the star of the biggest show in New York, the Ziegfeld Follies. He also began acting in silent films, which only increased his celebrity status. In his films, he sometimes portrayed cowboys, or perhaps comedic characters similar to himself. He continued acting in films up through 1935, eventually starring in over fifty movies.

Words to watch for:
enduring   sophisticated
relevant   syndicated

Rogers also started writing weekly newspaper columns in 1926. Over the course of his writing career, Will wrote more than 4,000 columns which were syndicated in newspapers all over the world. Additionally, he hosted a weekly radio program in which he told jokes and discussed many different issues that were relevant to people of that time period.

One of Will's favorite topics was the advancement of commercial aviation. He believed that airplanes were the future of travel, and he spoke about the subject frequently. He flew to every destination he could in an effort to prove how safe traveling by plane could be.

It was this love of aviation which eventually caused his death. In 1935, he embarked on a journey with his good friend Wiley Post (a pilot who had become famous for flying around the world). The two were attempting to fly over the Bering Strait from Alaska to Russia. Somewhere over Alaska, their motor stalled and the plane crashed, killing both men. Will Rogers' death was mourned by the entire nation. Kings and presidents from foreign nations even expressed their regrets at his passing.

Today, Will Rogers is remembered as an American legend. Buildings, streets, and even an airport have been named in his honor. There is also a statue of him standing in the U.S. Capital Building.

Multiple Choice: *Select the choice that completes the statement or answers the question.*

1._____ Which of the following best summarizes how Will Rogers became famous in South Africa, Australia, and New Zealand?
a. He ran for office and was elected mayor and then to Parliament.
b. He recorded several songs which became popular on South African radio.
c. He wrote a book which was a bestseller in all three nations.
d. He performed for a wild west show and then was hired by a circus.

2._____ Which of the following best describes why New York audiences loved Will Rogers?
a. They loved his country accent and his natural sense of humor.
b. They loved his rope tricks because they had never seen anything like it before.
c. They loved the fact that he gave away large amounts of candy at each performance.
d. They loved that he could sing, dance, tell jokes, and juggle as well.

3._____ Which of the following statements is false?
a. Will Rogers was starring in the Ziegfeld Follies in 1916.
b. Will Rogers starred in more than fifty films.
c. Will Rogers wrote more than 40,000 newspaper columns in his life.
d. Will Rogers hosted a weekly radio program.

4._____ Which of the following best describes Will Rogers' attitude towards flying?
a. He was terrified of flying and insisted on driving everywhere he went.
b. He was a strong advocate of commercial aviation and flew every chance he got.
c. He felt that flying was a fad and would never replace the train for traveling.
d. He did not have strong opinions about issues such as flying or commercial aviation.

5._____ Which of the following best summarizes Will Rogers' death?
a. He died after being diagnosed with bone cancer.
b. He was hit by an automobile while attempting to cross the street in New York City.
c. He died in an airplane crash, along with his friend Wiley Post.
d. He drowned in a shipwreck while his ocean liner was crossing the Atlantic.

©Reading Through History

Guided Reading: *Fill in the blanks below to create complete sentences.*

1. Will Rogers' parents were both part _____.

2. In 1901, Will Rogers and a friend moved to _____.

3. In Texas Jack's Wild West Show, Rogers performed as
"_____".

4. In 1904, Rogers returned to the United States and started performing _____
in New York City.

5. Rogers performed _____ and told jokes to the audience.

6. By 1916, Will Rogers was the star of the biggest show in New York, the
_____.

7. Will Rogers wrote more than 4,000 columns which were syndicated in newspapers all over
the _____.

8. Will Rogers believed that _____ were the future of travel.

9. In 1935, Rogers embarked on a journey with _____, flying across
the Bering Strait.

10. There is a _____ of Will Rogers standing in the U.S. Capital Building.

Vocabulary: *Match each word with its correct definition. Consider how the word is used in the lesson. This might help you define each term. Use a dictionary to help if necessary.*

a. enduring
b. sophisticated
c. relevant
d. syndicated
e. vaudeville

11._____ lasting or permanent

12._____ a variety show featuring comedians, dancers, singers, and other performers

13._____ someone who has experience and education; a socialite; high class

14._____ an article or column that is published in multiple places at the same time

15._____ something important or connected to something else

Summarize: *Answer the following questions in the space provided. Attempt to respond in a complete sentence for each question. Be sure to use correct capitalization and punctuation!*

1. Who was Will Rogers with when he died?

2. What was the name Will Rogers used while performing with Texas Jack's Wild West Show?

3. When did Will Rogers die?

4. Where did Will Rogers live when he was not in the United States? (Which nations did he spend time in?)

5. Why did Will Rogers fly everywhere he went?

6. How would Will Rogers open each show?

Student Response: *Be sure to use complete sentences!*

7. Will Rogers was extremely well-known for his humorous sayings. Using an outside resource, such as the internet, find a list of Will Rogers quotes and list five that you enjoy. Why did you enjoy them?

Wiley Post

Wiley Post was more than just an aviation superstar—he was also an innovator who advanced the science of flying. What did he do to become such a famous flyer?

Wiley Post saw an airplane for the first time when he was 15 years old. From that moment on, he wanted to fly. In the 1920s, he became a well-known "barnstorming" pilot. These were pilots who traveled around the country in flying circuses, performing dangerous stunts with airplanes.

However, in 1926, he was working in an oilfield when an accident occurred. Wiley was injured in the accident and lost his left eye. It briefly appeared that his flying career might be over, but he learned how to fly with the use of only one eye.

Post first gained national attention in 1930 when he won a cross-continent race in his plane, the *Winnie Mae*. He made the trip from Los Angeles to Chicago in 9 hours and 8 minutes.

In 1931, Post decided to fly around the world. He and his copilot left on June 23 and returned to their starting point on July 1st. The trip had taken eight days, 15 hours, and 51 minutes. This shattered the previous record of 21 days (which was set flying a zeppelin). Two years later, he decided to fly around the world again, only this time, he would go by himself. He became the first man to fly solo around the world, accomplishing the task in 7 days, 18 hours, and 49 minutes. This beat his old record by nearly an entire day!

The next year, Wiley began inventing a pressurized flight suit. Many others were also working on the idea. Everyone knew that such a suit would allow pilots to fly to much higher altitudes than ever before. He eventually constructed a suit with financial support from Frank Phillips (of Phillips Petroleum). The suit was made of rubber, with pigskin gloves, rubber boots, and a helmet made of plastic and aluminum. On his first successful test of the pressurized suit, he flew to an altitude of 40,000 feet. When one considers the number of ways this technology has been adapted in today's world, this was a remarkable achievement. The use of pressurized suits even helped us go to the moon!

> *Words to watch for:*
>
> *constructed   adapted*
>
> *pressurized   innovator*

During one of his test flights for the pressurized suit, Post began noticing that his groundspeed greatly exceeded his airspeed. This realization eventually led to the discovery of the jet stream. Today, the jet stream is widely used in commercial airline travel. It cuts travel time from Tokyo to Honolulu from 18 hours to 11.5 hours (as well as saving quite a bit of fuel). Meteorologists also use the jet stream to help forecast the weather more accurately.

Wiley Post died in 1935 while on a flight with Will Rogers. Their plane crashed on August 15, over Point Barrow, Alaska. Millions of people mourned the death of this famous flyer.

Today, the *Winnie Mae* is on display at the Smithsonian's National Air and Space Museum. Wiley Post has been commemorated on postage stamps and he has an airport named in his honor. He received the Distinguished Flying Cross, the Gold Medal of Belgium, and he's in the National Aviation Hall of Fame.

Multiple Choice: *Select the choice that completes the statement or answers the question.*

1._____ How did Wiley Post lose the use of his left eye?
a. He had a disease which infected his eye.
b. He lost it an oilfield accident.
c. He was born blind in that eye.
d. He lost it an airplane crash.

2._____ Why was Wiley Post's first flight around the world important?
a. He established a new world record. c. He only refueled the airplane once.
b. He made the flight without stopping. d. He won a race with other pilots.

3._____ Which of the following made Wiley Post's second flight around the world
even more impressive?
a. He made the flight without stopping. c. He made the flight solo.
b. He only refueled the airplane once. d. He won a race with other pilots.

4._____ What would a pressurized suit allow pilots to do?
a. stay in the air for longer periods of time
b. pilots would be able to fly upside down
c. pilots would be able to sleep while flying
d. fly higher than they had ever flown before

5._____ How did Wiley Post die?
a. he died of natural causes, in his sleep c. he died in a plane crash
b. he was killed in a shipwreck d. he was shot by rival pilots

Vocabulary: *Match each word with its correct definition. Consider how the word is used in the lesson. This might help you define each term. Use a dictionary to help if necessary.*

a. construct   d. commemorate
b. adapt   e. meteorologist
c. pressurized

6._____ to build or create by putting parts together

7._____ maintaining an air pressure comfortable for breathing

8._____ to adjust to different conditions

9._____ to honor the memory of

10._____ a scientist who studies the weather

Reading Comprehension & More: *Select the choice that answers the question.*

1._____ Which of the following best describes the main idea of this lesson?
a. Wiley Post was the most famous pilot who has ever lived.
b. Wiley Post's only achievement was winning a cross-continent race.
c. Wiley Post did many different things to help advance the science of flying.
d. Wiley Post's greatest achievement was being the first to fly around the world.

2._____ Which of the following sentences best supports the main idea of this lesson?
a. Wiley was injured in the accident and lost his left eye.
b. Post first gained national attention in 1930.
c. He won a cross-continent race in his plane, the *Winnie Mae*.
d. The next year, Wiley began inventing a pressurized flight suit.

3._____ Based on the information in the seventh paragraph, which of the following is
         probably the most accurate definition for "jet stream"?
a. The exhaust coming from the engine of a jet airplane.
b. A belt of high altitude winds moving at high speeds.
c. A narrow river of water with an extremely rapid current.
d. A factory that assembles jets and other aircraft.

4._____ Based on the information provided in this lesson, which of the following is most
         likely the best definition of "innovator"?
a. One who introduces something new; one who tries different things.
b. Someone who maintains to tried and true methods.
c. One who speaks out vocally and stands up for what he believes in.
d. Someone who creates a business and profits off of his product.

Guided Reading: *Fill in the blanks below to create complete sentences.*

5. Barnstorming pilots traveled around the country in flying circuses, performing dangerous
stunts with _____.

6. Wiley Post learned how to fly with the use of only one _____.

7. Post first gained national attention in 1930 when he won a cross-continent race in his plane,
the _____.

8. The pressurized suit Wiley Post created was made of rubber, with pigskin gloves, rubber
boots, and a helmet made of plastic and _____.

9. Post also discovered the _____ which is widely used in commercial
airline travel.

10.Today, the *Winnie Mae* is on display at the _____ National Air and Space
Museum.

Summarize: *Answer the following questions in the space provided.*
Attempt to respond in a complete sentence for each question.
Be sure to use correct capitalization and punctuation!

1. Who was with Wiley Post when his plane crashed?

2. What was the name of the plane Wiley Post flew in the cross-continent race?

3. When did Wiley Post fly around the world for the first time?

4. Where did Wiley Post die?

5. Why was the discovery of the jet-stream so important?

6. How did Wiley Post discover the jet-stream?

Student Response: *Write a paragraph addressing the questions raised below. A thorough response should consist of three to five complete sentences.*

7. Wiley Post died in a plane crash with Will Rogers. You have already read about both Will Rogers and Wiley Post. Which of these two figures do you feel was more important to society? Defend your answer.

Woody Guthrie

Unquestionably, the most enduring musical figure to emerge from the Dust Bowl era was a man named Woody Guthrie. Why was Woody so popular? What kind of songs did he sing?

Woody Guthrie was born in Okemah, Oklahoma in 1912. His father was the first County Clerk in Okfuskee County. By the standards of the day, his family was an average, middle-class family.

At the age of six, Woody's sister died tragically in a kitchen accident. Not long after, his mother was stricken with Huntington's disease. Doctors of the time were unfamiliar with the disease, and as a result, she was placed in a mental institution.

When Woody was 19, he moved to Pampa, Texas and started performing with a band known as the Corn Cob Trio. However, in 1935, he packed up his belongings and headed west with the rest of the "Okies".

Along the way, he rode in box cars and jalopies, going from Oklahoma, to Kansas, Colorado, and California. During his journeys, he lived amongst the migrant workers, singing to them and about them. He sang to people who were always too hot, too cold, too hungry, or too poor. He sang old hymns and folk songs, which comforted the migrants and reminded them of home and of simpler times.

He also wrote his own music. Many of the songs he wrote were hard-hitting social commentaries about what he saw going on around him: the hardships people were facing, the unemployment, the hunger, and the diseases which ravaged them.

As time progressed, the themes in his songs continued to become increasingly politicized. Much of his music advocated the sharing of wealth. He eventually became famous as a voice for the working class and a champion of worker rights. Many criticized his songs for these themes, and some even accused him of being a communist.

Woody genuinely believed in the ideals he sang about. He didn't believe in the personal ownership of his own music. He always said, "These songs didn't cost me anything to write, so you can have 'em if you want 'em." He also gave much of the money he made to those who needed it.

Throughout his years living in California amongst the migrant workers, he held many different jobs. He painted signs, picked fruit, and washed dishes. He hosted a weekly radio show out of Los Angeles where he was billed as "Oklahoma Woody". He even wrote a weekly newspaper column called "Woody Sez..."

In 1940, Woody left California and traveled to New York City. It was there that he wrote his most famous song "This Land is Your Land" as a protest song. It was also in New York where he finally recorded many of the songs he had been singing for years. RCA made a collection of Woody Guthrie music known as _Dust Bowl Ballads_.

> _Words to watch for:_
>
> _jalopies   advocated_
>
> _communist   protest_

Unfortunately for Woody, he began exhibiting some of the early symptoms of Huntington's disease, the same illness which had inflicted his mother. By the early 1950s, his condition was so bad that he was no longer able to perform, and he spent the final years of his life in and out of the hospital. He died in 1967 at the age of 55.

Woody Guthrie changed the world of American music forever. He was one of the first extremely influential singer-songwriters in American history. He inspired countless other songwriters who followed him, and he continues to do so today.

Multiple Choice: *Select the choice that completes the statement or answers the question.*

1._____ Which of the following significant events occurred in Woody Guthrie's life in 1935?
a. His sister died.
b. He moved to California.
c. His mother died.
d. He got married.

2._____ Which of the following best describes why Woody Guthrie sang old folk songs and hymns?
a. These were the only songs he was familiar with.
b. He did not believe in writing his own music.
c. He believed that these were the best songs ever written.
d. The songs reminded his audience of home and simpler times.

3._____ Which of the following best summarizes why some were critical of Woody Guthrie's music?
a. Many felt that his songs advocated the sharing of wealth.
b. Many felt that his songs were not catchy enough to be popular.
c. Many felt that his songs were too warm-hearted and were not appropriate during the Great Depression.
d. Many felt that his songs would have sounded better if sung by someone else.

4._____ Which of the following best summarizes Woody Guthrie's attitude towards song ownership?
a. He charged hefty fees for anyone who wanted to sing one of his songs.
b. He insisted that he was the only one who could sing a song he had written.
c. He did not believe in the ownership of songs and let anyone record his music.
d. He had little to do with his own music after he wrote the songs, so it was not an issue.

5._____ Which of the following is an opinion?
a. RCA released a collection of Woody Guthrie music known as *Dust Bowl Ballads*.
b. Woody Guthrie started exhibiting symptoms of Huntington's disease in the 1950s.
c. Woody Guthrie is the most influential singer-songwriter who ever lived.
d. "This Land is Your Land" was written as a protest song.

Guided Reading: *Fill in the blanks below to create complete sentences.*

1. Woody Guthrie was born in _____, Oklahoma in 1912.

2. When Woody was 19, he moved to _____, Texas.

3. During his journeys, Woody Guthrie lived amongst the migrant _____, singing to them and about them.

4. Many of the songs he wrote were hard-hitting social _____ about what he saw going on around him.

5. Woody Guthrie eventually became famous as a voice for the working class and a champion of _____.

6. Woody gave much of the _____ he made as an artist to those who needed it.

7. Guthrie hosted a weekly radio show out of Los Angeles, where he was billed as "_____ Woody".

8. Woody Guthrie wrote his most famous song, _____, in 1940.

9. Woody Guthrie died in 1967, at the age of _____.

10. Woody Guthrie changed the world of American _____ forever.

Vocabulary: *Match each word with its correct definition. Consider how the word is used in the lesson. This might help you define each term. Use a dictionary to help if necessary.*

a. jalopy   d. protest
b. advocate   e. exhibit
c. communist

11. _____ a battered old automobile

12._____ to manifest or display

13._____ one who opposes the private ownership of property and businesses

14._____ speaking or writing in support of one cause or another

15._____ an expression of disapproval or dissent against someone or something

Summarize: *Answer the following questions in the space provided. Attempt to respond in a complete sentence for each question. Be sure to use correct capitalization and punctuation!*

1. Which of Woody's relatives had Huntington's disease?

2. What was the title of Woody Guthrie's most famous song?

3. When did Woody Guthrie leave Pampa, Texas for California?

4. Where did Woody Guthrie go in 1940?

5. Why was Woody Guthrie unable to perform in the early 1950s?

6. How is Woody Guthrie remembered today?

Student Response: *Write a paragraph addressing the questions raised below. A thorough response should consist of three to five complete sentences.*

7. How do you think Woody Guthrie would feel about modern day issues such as file-sharing and music piracy? Cite specific evidence from the text to support your argument.

Pretty Boy Floyd

*In the late 1920s and 1930s, there were several notorious
outlaws roaming the countryside. One of the most famous of
these outlaws was Pretty Boy Floyd. Why was Floyd so
famous? Why was he called Pretty Boy?*

On February 3rd, 1904, Charles Arthur Floyd was born on a
cold day in Georgia. He was the fourth of what would
eventually be eight children in the Floyd family. In 1911,
Charles' father moved the family to eastern Oklahoma, hoping
to earn a living picking cotton. They settled down in a region
commonly known as the Cookson Hills. This was where
Charles grew up. By all accounts, he was a good kid and many
people liked him.

When Charles was fifteen, he worked with a harvest crew that traveled the area. Many
of the harvesters were rough individuals with criminal backgrounds. Charles listened
with interest to their stories of adventure and making money "the easy way". Then, one
night in 1922, Charles and a friend broke into the local post office, robbing it of every
penny they could find. They acquired $3.50.

Even though he made little money, his appetite for crime had been encouraged, and he
did not enjoy the hard labor of the cotton fields. So, he moved to St. Louis where he
began a life of crime, robbing from gas stations and grocery stores. At one store, he
made away with over $11,500. One of the newspapers that reported the event quoted a
witness who said that Charles looked like "a mere boy, with apple cheeks—a real pretty
boy." The nickname stuck, and from then on, Charles Floyd became known as Pretty
Boy Floyd.

The authorities tracked him down, and Floyd was sentenced to prison. Prison life was
miserable. He shared a cell with seven other inmates and frequently heard stories about
others being beaten, strangled, or stabbed in their sleep. As a result, he didn't sleep
much. While in prison, he was told by other inmates that when he was released, he
should go to Kansas City, which he did.

Words to watch for:
notorious   resumed
sentenced   incident

He resumed his criminal career from there, traveling all
across the Midwest, from Missouri to New York. One day,
while in Akron, Ohio, Floyd and his associates were hiding
out in a motel when they were surprised by the authorities.
Pretty Boy was captured and sentenced to fifteen years in
prison.

As he was being transferred from jail to prison, Floyd asked the guard to remove his
handcuffs so he could use the restroom. The guard agreed. Moments later, Charles
made a daring escape by crawling out of a small bathroom window. The next day, the
newspaper headlines announced "Pretty Boy Escapes Train to Prison!" Floyd hated his
new nickname—but he loved all the attention.

Not long after, law enforcement agents once again caught up to Floyd, this time in Toledo, Ohio. Pretty Boy was able to make yet another miraculous escape. He sped off in his car, driving across sidewalks, through lawns, and down alleys before finally getting away.

By this time, it was 1931 and Floyd returned to his home in the Cookson Hills. He was shocked to discover how hard the Great Depression had hit eastern Oklahoma and how much it had affected his friends and area families. He decided that he would do what he could to help. So, he did the only thing he knew.

In 1931-32, Pretty Boy Floyd began robbing banks all over Oklahoma. Some legends claim that he robbed as many as fifty-one banks in 1931 alone. Much of the money he stole, he sent back to the families of the Cookson Hills. He bought food and clothing for those in need. He made Christmas possible for families that otherwise would not have had one.

For many, he became a Robin Hood-like figure, "robbing from the rich and giving to the poor". However, the state of Oklahoma, and the Federal Bureau of Investigation, saw things differently. A price was placed on his capture, $6,000 dead or alive.

On June 17th, 1933, Pretty Boy was accused of an incident known as the Kansas City Massacre. Four police officers had been murdered, and Pretty Boy received the blame. He protested his innocence in the crime, even sending a letter to the Kansas City Police Department. His letter said "Dear Sirs, I Charles Floyd, want it made known that I did not participate in the massacre of officers at Kansas City." Many historians agree that Floyd probably did not kill the officers in question. However, this earned him the #2 spot on the FBI's "Public Enemies" list, behind only John Dillinger.

Finally, on October 19th, 1934, Pretty Boy was spotted on the side of the road near Clarkson, Ohio after he had accidentally wrecked his automobile. Law enforcement officials chased Floyd, who was primarily on foot, for several days before they tracked him down in a cornfield. He was shot and killed on October 22nd while attempting to run away.

Floyd's body was returned to the Cookson Hills. His funeral was held in Sallisaw, Oklahoma and was attended by anywhere from 20,000 to 40,000 people. To this day, it remains the largest funeral in the history of the state.

Despite his life of crime, the character of Pretty Boy Floyd has lived on in the imagination of the culture. In 1939, Woody Guthrie sang "The Ballad of Pretty Boy Floyd" which became an incredibly popular song and helped nurture the outlaw's legend. He has been the subject of many books (both historical and fiction), and his life and death have been portrayed multiple times on film.

Multiple Choice: *Select the choice that completes the statement or answers the question.*

1._____ Which of the following best summarizes why the Floyd family moved to the Cookson Hills?
a. His father was a wanted criminal, and they thought they would find safety there.
b. His father was hoping to make a living by picking cotton.
c. His mother wanted her children to be closer to their grandparents.
d. His mother was sick and needed to be closer to a doctor who could treat her.

2._____ Which of the following best describes how Charles Floyd acquired the nickname "Pretty Boy"?
a. This was a nickname he chose himself, so he would stand out from other criminals.
b. He was extremely vain, always combing his hair and looking in the mirror.
c. He was often mistaken for a woman.
d. An eyewitness described him as "a mere boy with apple cheeks, a real pretty boy."

3._____ Which of the following best describes what Pretty Boy Floyd did with much of the money he stole?
a. He buried large portions of his money at Robber's Cave.
b. He always spent the money quickly, throwing lavish parties for his friends.
c. He gave large portions of the money to the starving people of the Cookson Hills.
d. He turned the money over to the authorities in exchange for a lighter prison sentence.

4._____ Which of the following incidents was Pretty Boy Floyd accused of being involved in?
a. The Kansas City Massacre   c. The Sand Creek Massacre
b. The St. Valentine's Day Massacre   d. The Wounded Knee Massacre

5._____ Which of the following statements is *not* true?
a. Woody Guthrie wrote "The Ballad of Pretty Boy Floyd" which became a popular song.
b. There have been many books written about the life of Pretty Boy Floyd.
c. There is a statue dedicated to Pretty Boy Floyd in the Oklahoma State Capital Building.
d. Pretty Boy Floyd's life and death have been portrayed multiple times on film.

Vocabulary: *Match each word with its correct definition. Consider how the word is used in the lesson. This might help you define each term. Use a dictionary to help if necessary.*

a. notorious
b. resume
c. sentence
d. incident
e. nurture

6._____ to feed and encourage; promote the development of

7._____ widely known for negative reasons

8._____ an individual occurrence or event

9._____ to continue on with, usually after an interruption

10._____ a judgment which determines the punishment to be inflicted

Guided Reading: *Fill in the blanks below to create complete sentences.*

1. One night in 1922, Charles and a friend broke into the local
_____, robbing it of every penny they could find.

2. Charles Floyd moved to St. Louis where he began a life of _____.

3. While in prison, Floyd was told by other inmates that when he was released, he
should go to _____.

4. Charles made a daring escape by crawling out of a small bathroom
_____.

5. In 1931, Floyd returned to his home in the Cookson Hills and was shocked to discover
how hard the _____ had hit eastern Oklahoma.

6. Some legends claim that Floyd robbed as many as _____ banks in
1931 alone.

7. For many, he became a _____-like figure, "robbing from the
rich and giving to the poor".

8. Floyd was #2 on the FBI's "_____" list, behind
only John Dillinger.

9. Law enforcement officials chased Floyd, who was primarily _____,
for several days before they tracked him down in a cornfield.

10. Floyd's funeral was attended by anywhere from 20,000 to _____ people.

Summarize: *Answer the following questions in the space provided. Attempt to respond in a complete sentence for each question. Be sure to use correct capitalization and punctuation!*

1. Who was ahead of Pretty Boy Floyd on the FBI's "Public Enemies" list?

2. What did Charles Floyd hear stories about while working with harvest crews?

3. When did Pretty Boy Floyd die? (date and year)

4. Where did Charles Floyd grow up?

5. Why did Floyd decide to give the money he stole to the people of the Cookson Hills?

6. How did Pretty Boy Floyd die?

Student Response: *Write a paragraph addressing the questions raised below. A thorough response should consist of three to five complete sentences.*

7. Pretty Boy Floyd was a criminal who robbed banks. Do you think it's wrong to celebrate such a figure? Or do you feel that his charitable actions toward the people of the Cookson Hills area outweigh his wrongdoing? Explain your answer as thoroughly as possible.

Unit Four:
Modern Oklahoma

45th Infantry Thunderbird Division

During World War II, the Thunderbirds became a well-known infantry division. Who were the Thunderbirds? What did they do to gain such recognition?

In October of 1920, the Oklahoma state militia was organized into the 45th Infantry Division of the Oklahoma National Guard. Three years later, in 1923, it was recognized federally as a National Guard unit. However, they did not become known by the name Thunderbirds until 1939, when they adopted a new shoulder insignia. The logo featured a golden Native American thunderbird on a red field. This symbol eventually became synonymous with the 45th Infantry.

The 45th was not used in combat until the outbreak of World War II. On September 16, 1941, the 45th Infantry was federalized. This meant they were turned over from state control to regular army control. They were sent to Fort Sill to begin combat training immediately.

By the time the Thunderbirds arrived in North Africa, Allied forces had already secured most of the African front. It would not be long, however, before the 45th Infantry saw their share of action. Throughout the final two years of the war, the 45th participated in the invasion of Sicily, the advance through Italy, and the Battle of Anzio. They also helped liberate France and pursue the Nazis into Germany during the final stages of the war. The Thunderbirds also participated in the liberation of the Dachau concentration camp and were responsible for the capture of more than 124,000 German soldiers.

Some members of the 45th Infantry were Native Americans. The military utilized their skills in native languages to better communicate via radio. These code talkers would relay messages in Cherokee, Choctaw, Cheyenne, Kiowa, Seminole, Comanche, and many other Native American languages. The Nazis were unable to decipher these languages, and the code talkers proved to be a major contribution to the eventual Allied victory. Because of the unit's effectiveness in combat and unique skillsets, US Army General George S. Patton declared that the 45th Infantry was "one of the best, if not the best division in the history of American arms."

> *Words to watch for:*
>
> *infantry synonymous*
>
> *militia stalemate*

The 45th Infantry was reactivated during the Korean Conflict in 1951. They saw significant fighting in Korea during the long stalemate in the second half of the war. The Thunderbirds were finally deactivated in 1968 as part of a nationwide effort to reduce the size of the National Guard. Throughout its history, the 45th Infantry sustained more than 25,000 casualties in battle and had nine Medal of Honor winners amongst its ranks.

Multiple Choice: *Select the choice that completes the statement or answers the question.*

1._____ Which of the following best describes how the 45th Infantry Division of the
Oklahoma National Guard became known as the Thunderbirds?
a. This was a nickname designated to them when they became federally recognized in 1923.
b. The division earned this nickname after a fierce battle at Thunderbird Island.
c. The division's original headquarters was located near Lake Thunderbird.
d. The name was adopted after they began wearing a shoulder insignia featuring a golden bird.

2._____ Which of the following events did the 45th Infantry *not* participate in?
a. the invasion of Sicily   c. the liberation of France
b. the Battle of Iwo Jima   d. the liberation of Dachau

3._____ Which of the following contributions did Native Americans make to the war effort?
a. They volunteered their services as scouts and spies, providing important information to
Allied soldiers.
b. They acted as negotiators between the Allied and Axis Powers at the end of the war.
c. They used their native languages to communicate via radio, which created a code the Nazis
were unable to break.
d. They trained troops throughout the war, teaching them native tactics in stealth and secrecy.

4._____ Which of the following best summarizes why the 45th Infantry was disbanded?
a. It was part of a nationwide effort to reduce the size of the national guard.
b. It was disbanded at the conclusion of World War II because it was no longer needed.
c. It was decided that individual states no longer needed their own national guard divisions.
d. It was determined that the 45th Infantry had been ineffective in combat, so its members
were assigned to other divisions.

5._____ Which of the following statements about the 45th Infantry is *not* accurate?
a. The 45th Infantry was reactivated during the Korean Conflict.
b. The 45th Infantry sustained more than 25,000 casualties in battle.
c. The 45th Infantry became known as the Lightning Division.
d. The 45th Infantry had nine Medal of Honor winners.

Vocabulary: *Match each word with its correct definition. Consider how the word is used in the lesson.*
This might help you define each term. Use a dictionary to help if necessary.

a. infantry   d. synonymous
b. insignia   e. stalemate
c. militia

6._____ a situation in which no action is being taken; deadlock

7._____ soldiers that fight on foot, typically with rifles or machine guns

8._____ closely associated with; implying the same idea

9._____ a distinguishing mark or symbol which stands for something else

10._____ a body of regular citizens enrolled for military service; not professional soldiers

Guided Reading: *Fill in the blanks below to create complete sentences.*

1. The Oklahoma state militia was organized into the 45th Infantry Division of the Oklahoma _____.

2. The 45th was not used in combat until the outbreak of _____.

3. Throughout the final two years of WWII, the 45th participated in the invasion of Sicily, the advance through Italy, and the Battle of _____.

4. Code talkers would relay messages in Cherokee, Choctaw, Cheyenne, Kiowa, Seminole, _____ and many other Native American languages.

5. The 45th Infantry saw significant fighting in _____ during the second half of the war.

Correct the Statement: *Each of the following sentences is false. Circle the incorrect word and write the word or phrase that makes the statement correct in the answer blank provided.*

6. In 1941, the 45th Infantry was sent to Fort Bragg to begin combat training immediately. _____.

7. The 45th Infantry pursued the Nazis into Russia during the final stages of the war. _____.

8. All members of the 45th Infantry were Native Americans. _____.

9. The code talkers proved to be a major contribution to the eventual Axis victory. _____.

10. The 45th Infantry Division was reactivated during the Vietnam Conflict. _____.

Summarize: *Answer the following questions in the space provided. Attempt to respond in a complete sentence for each question. Be sure to use correct capitalization and punctuation!*

1. Who utilized their language as code to communicate via radio?

2. What was the nickname used by the 45th Infantry?

3. When was the 45th Infantry federalized for use in World War II?

4. Which concentration camp did the 45th Infantry help liberate?

5. Why were the native languages so effective to use as codes?

6. How many Medal of Honor winners were there in the 45th Infantry?

Student Response: *Write a paragraph addressing the questions raised below. A thorough response should consist of three to five complete sentences.*

7. Paragraphs four and five of the lesson describe many of the 45th Infantry Division's accomplishments. Of these, which do you feel benefited the war effort the most? Justify your answer, and explain as thoroughly as possible.

Oklahoma!

One of the most successful musicals of all time is Oklahoma! *Why is this musical so well-known? How has it altered the nation's perception of the state?*

In the early 1940s, Richard Rodgers and Oscar Hammerstein wanted to write a musical based on a stage play titled *Green Grow the Lilacs*. The setting for the play was just outside the town of Claremore in Oklahoma Territory in 1906. It tells the story of a romance between a cowboy, Curly McLain, and a farmer girl, Laurey Williams.

Prior to putting their musical on Broadway, the duo tested the show, which was titled *Away We Go!* in other markets. Crowds in Boston, Massachusetts and New Haven, Connecticut were both enthusiastic. However, it was given lukewarm reviews from critics. Rogers and Hammerstein felt there was still something missing. Prior to its release on Broadway, the duo made two crucial changes. First, they added a show-stopping song & dance number titled "Oklahoma!" Additionally, they changed the title of the musical to match the new song.

Oklahoma! debuted on Broadway in the St. James Theater on March 31, 1943. It was an instant success with both New York audiences and critics. The production would eventually run for an astounding five years and 2,212 performances. During this time, it grossed more than $7 million in box office revenue. There was also a national tour with live performances across the country. By the early 1950s, more than 20 million viewers had seen *Oklahoma!*

In 1955, *Oklahoma!* made its way onto the silver screen. A film adaptation of the stage musical only increased the show's popularity. This film version would eventually win three Academy Awards, including the award for Best Music.

> *Words to watch for:*
>
> perception   lukewarm
>
> crucial   colloquial

Oklahoma! produced some of the most beloved songs in the history of musicals. "Oh, What a Beautiful Morning", "Surrey With a Fringe on Top", "Kansas City", "I Cain't Say No", and of course, the title song "Oklahoma!" are all thought of as classics. In 1953, the state of Oklahoma adopted "Oklahoma!" as its official state song. To this day, it remains one of the most instantly recognizable official state songs.

The state of Oklahoma has both embraced the musical and attempted to distance itself from the stigma associated with it. The incredible popularity of the show has generated much interest, name recognition, and tourism for the state over the years. However, many non-Oklahomans are left with a stereotypical view that all Oklahomans are cowboys and farmhands who speak with colloquial accents.

In the years since it was first on Broadway, *Oklahoma!* has achieved legendary status. It is regarded as one of the most influential Broadway musicals of all time. Some historians view it as the first truly musical play that blends song, dance, characters, and plot. It became the model for all future Broadway shows, as well as the standard by which those shows were compared.

Multiple Choice: *Select the choice that completes the statement or answers the question.*

1._____ Which of the following duos is responsible for writing the musical *Oklahoma!*?
a. Porgy & Bess
b. Gilbert & Sullivan
c. Rodgers & Hammerstein
d. Sherman & Sherman

2._____ Which of the following best describes how *Oklahoma!* was received when it initially opened on Broadway?
a. It was an instant success with both audiences and critics.
b. It was an instant success with audiences, but critics did not like it.
c. At first, many audiences did not understand it, but it slowly found its supporters.
d. At first, audiences liked it, but quickly tired of the actors' unconvincing performances.

3._____ Which of the following songs is *not* from the musical *Oklahoma!*
a. "Oh What a Beautiful Morning"
b. "This Land is Your Land"
c. "Surrey With a Fringe on Top"
d. "Kansas City"

4._____ Which of the following statements is most accurate?
a. The musical *Oklahoma!* has not benefited the state in any way.
b. Many Oklahomans do not like the stereotypes that have been created by *Oklahoma!*
c. Most Oklahomans do not like the song *Oklahoma!* because they feel it is overplayed.
d. Most Oklahomans have performed in a live version of *Oklahoma!* at some point in their life.

5._____ Which of the following statements is not accurate?
a. *Oklahoma!* was once very popular, but it is rarely performed today.
b. *Oklahoma!* is regarded as one of the most influential Broadway musicals of all time.
c. *Oklahoma!* is viewed by some historians as the first truly musical play.
d. *Oklahoma!* has become the standard by which all Broadway shows are compared.

Vocabulary: *Match each word with its correct definition. Consider how the word is used in the lesson. This might help you define each term. Use a dictionary to help if necessary.*

a. perception
b. lukewarm
c. crucial
d. stigma
e. colloquial

6._____ the way one views or thinks about something

7._____ a mark of disgrace on one's reputation

8._____ the informal speech of casual conversation

9._____ showing little enthusiasm towards; halfhearted

10._____ extremely important

Guided Reading: *Fill in the blanks below to create complete sentences.*

1. *Oklahoma!* tells the story of a romance between a cowboy, _____, and a farmer girl, Laurey Williams.

2. When the musical was tested in Boston, Massachusetts and New Haven, Connecticut it was given lukewarm reviews from _____.

3. Prior to its release on Broadway, the show-stopping song & dance number titled "_____" was added to the musical.

4. *Oklahoma!* would eventually run for an astounding _____ years and 2,212 performances.

5. By the early 1950s, more than _____ viewers had seen *Oklahoma!*

6. In 1955, *Oklahoma!* made its way onto the _____.

7. This film version would eventually win three Academy Awards, including the award for _____.

8. In 1953, the state of Oklahoma adopted "Oklahoma!" as its official

_____.

9. The incredible popularity of the show has generated much interest, name recognition, and _____ for the state.

10. In the years since it was first on _____, *Oklahoma!* has achieved legendary status.

Summarize: *Answer the following questions in the space provided. Attempt to respond in a complete sentence for each question. Be sure to use correct capitalization and punctuation!*

1. Who wrote the musical *Oklahoma!*?

2. What was the original title of the stage play on which *Oklahoma!* is based?

3. When did *Oklahoma!* debut on Broadway?

4. Where do the events of *Oklahoma!* take place?

5. Why have some Oklahomans tried to distance themselves from the musical?

6. How has the musical benefited the state of Oklahoma?

Student Response: *Write a paragraph addressing the questions raised below. A thorough response should consist of three to five complete sentences.*

7. Have you ever seen a live performance of *Oklahoma!*? If so, describe the experience as best you can, using as much detail as possible. If not, would you like to? Why or why not? Explain your answer as thoroughly as possible.

Oil Boom and Bust

The state of Oklahoma has almost always been associated with oil. When did oil become a valuable part of the state's economy? Has the oil business always been so prosperous?

Early explorers and Native Americans had always known there was oil in Oklahoma. It could be seen in creeks and riverbeds as it seeped up to the surface. It was used as a lubricant as well as fuel for lanterns. Some also used the oil for medicinal purposes. It was not until the late 1800s and early 1900s when there was a high demand for the product. The invention of the automobile and the internal combustion engine made oil one of the most valuable commodities on the planet.

The Nellie Johnstone No. 1, near Bartlesville, was the first commercial oil well drilled in Indian Territory. This well struck oil on April 15, 1897 and eventually produced more than 100,000 barrels of oil. Just a few years later, oil was discovered outside of Tulsa at the Red Fork Field. Then, in 1905, the Glen Pool became the first major oil field in the territory.

Not long after that, in 1912, Tom Slick (known as "King of the Wildcatters") and his partner, C.B. Shaffer, discovered the Cushing-Drumright Pool. By 1915, the Cushing field was producing more than 300,000 barrels of oil a day and was the nation's largest source of oil. Cushing became known as the "Pipeline Crossroads of the World."

> *Words to watch for:*
>
> *fledgling   recession*
>
> *scarce   revenue*

As the oil production in the new state continued to expand, thousands of oilfield workers flooded in to make Oklahoma their new home. The new arrivals meant more restaurants, hotels, saloons, schools, and churches. Tulsa was a booming city, and it wasn't long before it became thought of as the "Oil Capital of the World".

Frank Phillips, J.J. McAlester, Thomas Gilcrease, Robert S. Kerr, Erle Halliburton, E.W. Marland, and many others made their fortunes in the oilfields of Oklahoma. Additionally, the oil industry provided a strong foundation for the fledgling state's growing economy. Railroads, new highways, and other industries soon followed.

The early 1980s saw another oil boom in Oklahoma. It was an exciting time for the state, as the rest of the nation was experiencing a recession. The peak year of the boom was 1982. In January of that year, there were 882 active oil wells in the state.

Oil speculators and investors swarmed into Oklahoma, just as they had years before, hoping to strike it rich. New oilfields also meant thousands of workers taking up residence in the state. This created additional booms in the real estate market, as well as bringing in other new businesses. Schools were overcrowded and housing was scarce, as communities could not keep up with the growing demand.

Unfortunately, the prosperous times would not last. With so much oil on the market, the prices collapsed. The Oklahoma economy stuttered to a halt, and what was once a boom became a bust. The number of oil-related jobs in the state plummeted from 102,000 in 1982 to 46,000 in 1988. By 1986, there were only 170 oil rigs operating within the state. In just a few years, Oklahoma went from being the state with the lowest unemployment rate to the state with the highest.

The banking system was deeply impacted by the downturn. Throughout the boom, many banks had handed out large loans to oil-related companies. When these companies collapsed, they could not afford to pay back the loans. As a result, banks across the state began shutting down, including the Penn Square Bank which had more than $450 million in deposits. In 1987 alone, more than thirty-one banks shut their doors. By 1990, 1/5 of all Oklahoma banks had closed.

Most of those who had come to Oklahoma for work in the oilfields left the state in search of jobs. As the population decreased, this impacted other businesses, which no longer had as many customers. The state government was hurt as well, since less people meant less tax revenue.

However, the oil industry did not leave Oklahoma completely. In fact, Oklahoma is still one of the nation's leading producers in oil and other petroleum-based products. New technologies have allowed companies to drill for oil at deeper depths than was once possible. Oil will almost certainly continue to be the backbone of the state's economy for many years to come.

Multiple Choice: *Select the choice that completes the statement or answers the question.*

1._____ Which of the following is *not* mentioned as an early use for oil?
a. used as an ingredient in food   c. fuel for lanterns
b. it was used as a lubricant   d. medicinal purposes

2._____ Which of the following led to oil becoming one of the most valued commodities
          on the planet?
a. the increased use of oil lanterns to light homes in the evening
b. the discovery that oil could be used for medical treatments
c. the discovery of the chemical process which turns oil into rubber
d. the invention of the automobile and the internal combustion engine

3._____ Which of the following nicknames was Tulsa given?
a. "King of the Wildcatters"   c. "The Oil Capital of the World"
b. "The Pipeline Crossroads of the World" d. "The Wheat Capital of the World"

4._____ Why did oil prices collapse during the 1980s?
a. There was no longer a use for oil.
b. There was too much oil on the market.
c. Scientists had discovered that oil was hurting the environment.
d. New techniques had made drilling for oil obsolete.

5._____ Which of the following is *not* one of the ways that Oklahoma was hurt by the
          downturn in the oil market?
a. Many people lost their jobs and left the state.
b. Banks closed because businesses could not afford to pay back their loans.
c. Entrepreneurs began to view Oklahoma as an unlucky place to start a business.
d. State tax revenues went down because there were less people paying taxes.

Vocabulary: *Match each word with its correct definition. Consider how the word is used in the lesson. This might help you define each term. Use a dictionary to help if necessary.*

a. commodity   d. scarce
b. fledgling   e. revenue
c. recession

6._____ something that is young, new, or inexperienced

7._____ something of use or value

8._____ the amount of money regularly coming in

9._____ not enough to satisfy the demand or need

10._____ a temporary downturn in economic activity

Guided Reading: *Fill in the blanks below to create complete sentences.*

1. Early explorers and Native Americans had always known there was
_____ in Oklahoma.

2. Oil was discovered just outside of Tulsa at the _____
Field.

3. By 1915, the _____ field was producing more than
300,000 barrels of oil a day.

4. As the oil production continued to expand, thousands of oilfield workers
flooded in to make _____ their new home.

5. The oil industry provided a strong _____ for the
fledgling state's growing economy.

6. The early 1980s saw another oil boom for the state of Oklahoma, with the
peak year of the boom coming in _____.

7. Schools were _____ and housing was scarce as
communities could not keep up with the growing demand.

8. The number of oil-related jobs in the state plummeted from 102,000 in
1982 to _____ in 1988.

9. In 1987 alone, more than _____ banks shut their doors.

10. As the population decreased, this impacted other businesses, which no
longer had as many _____.

Summarize: *Answer the following questions in the space provided. Attempt to respond in a complete sentence for each question. Be sure to use correct capitalization and punctuation.*

1. Who was known as "King of the Wildcatters"?

2. What was the name of the first commercial oil well drilled in Indian Territory?

3. When did there become a high demand for oil?

4. Where was the "Pipeline Crossroads of the World"?

5. Why did many banks begin shutting down in the 1980s?

6. Which oilfield became the first major oilfield in the territory?

Student Response: *Write a paragraph addressing the questions raised below. A thorough response should consist of three to five complete sentences.*

7. Do you have any relatives who work in the oil industry? If so, who, and what is their occupation? If not, how might the oil industry impact your day-to-day life? Explain your answer thoroughly.

Name_____

Oil has always been an important part of Oklahoma's proud history. Utilize a map of Oklahoma and internet resources to help you locate and label the following places related to Oklahoma's oil industry.

Cities and towns should be labeled with a •

Bartlesville	Tulsa	Glenpool	McAlester (named for J.J. McAlester)
Cushing	Drumright	Red Fork	Ponca City (home of E.W. Marland)

The Oklahoma City Bombing

In the spring of 1995, a catastrophe occurred in Oklahoma City. What exactly happened that day? Who was responsible?

At 9:02 AM, on April 19th, 1995, a tremendous explosion shook Oklahoma City. Glass, granite, concrete, and steel rained down from the sky around the Alfred P. Murrah Federal Building. The blast was so powerful that street signs and parking meters had been ripped from the ground. Pedestrians were lifted off their feet and thrown across the sidewalk. Glass had been shattered in windows several blocks away.

The Murrah Building was almost completely destroyed. The devastation inside was horrific and survival was determined only by where an individual happened to be in the building at the time of the blast. The upper floors had collapsed upon the lower ones, leaving little chance for anyone on the ground level.

Rescue workers rushed to the scene and began searching for survivors. The work was dangerous due to the possibility that the rest of the building could collapse. However, rescue crews worked quickly to ensure that more lives would not be lost. By the time the rescue operations completed, 168 deaths (including 19 children) had been recorded, and more than 500 had been wounded.

While rescue workers searched for survivors, investigative teams were attempting to discover the cause of the explosion. Within minutes, the authorities realized that the source of the blast had been a 4,000 pound ammonium-nitrate bomb which had been hidden inside a Ryder truck.

Words to watch for:

catastrophe   conspirators

infringement   arraignment

At first, the investigators suspected the work of Middle East terrorists. Unfortunately, the eventual truth proved to be even more frightening. It was soon announced that the primary culprit was an American veteran named Tim McVeigh. He had been arrested in Perry, Oklahoma on an unrelated concealed weapons charge. He was in jail, awaiting arraignment when it was revealed that he was the primary suspect in the bombing investigation.

A US Army veteran of the Persian Gulf War, McVeigh was also a firearms enthusiast who enjoyed the outdoors and hunting. While in the military he had met Terry Nichols and Michael Fortier, the two men who became his co-conspirators in the bombing.

In 1993, the Bureau of Alcohol, Tobacco & Firearms had conducted a military-style siege of a compound owned by a religious group known as the Branch Davidians in Waco, Texas. McVeigh and Nichols saw this action as an infringement of civil liberties, so they devised a plan to retaliate. They had chosen the federal building in Oklahoma City as their target because they mistakenly believed that the ATF agents responsible for the raid were stationed there.

McVeigh, Nichols, and Fortier were all arrested and placed on trial for their involvement in the bombing of the Murrah Federal Building. Michael Fortier received 12 years in prison for his limited involvement in the plan. Terry Nichols was sentenced to life in prison, while Tim McVeigh was sentenced to death. McVeigh's sentence was carried out on June 11, 2001. He was the first prisoner to be executed by the federal government since 1963.

Multiple Choice: *Select the choice that completes the statement or answers the question.*

1._____ Which of the following correctly identifies the source of the explosion that destroyed the federal building in Oklahoma City?
a. a large gas leak that had gone unnoticed for several days
b. a small tactical nuclear device which was hidden inside a briefcase
c. a 4,000 pound ammonium-nitrate bomb hidden inside a Ryder truck
d. a case of dynamite which had been smuggled into the building

2._____ Which of the following most accurately describes the primary culprit in the Oklahoma City bombing?
a. a Middle Eastern jihadist who hated the United States
b. a former American soldier with a deep grudge against the United States
c. a schizophrenic loner who lived in a shack in the rural regions of Montana
d. a religious zealot who believed he was following instructions from a god

3._____ Those responsible for the Oklahoma City bombing saw their actions as retaliation for which of the following events?
a. A siege of the Branch Davidian compound in Waco, Texas, which had been conducted by members of the Bureau of Alcohol, Tobacco & Firearms.
b. The arrest of a major religious figure that had been inspirational to all three men involved.
c. The Gulf War which all three men had fought in, but viewed as an unjust war against a nation who had caused no harm to the United States.
d. The enforcement of laws which they felt were in violation of their First Amendment right to freedom of speech.

4._____ Which of the following reasons best explains why the federal building in Oklahoma City was targeted?
a. They believed it would be much more of a challenge to attack a target in Oklahoma City than in Washington D.C.
b. They believed that those who had arrested their religious leader were stationed in Oklahoma City.
c. They believed the general responsible for initiating the Gulf War had recently been transferred to Oklahoma City.
d. They believed that the ATF agents responsible for the Branch Davidian raid were stationed there.

5._____ Which of the following statements is inaccurate?
a. Michael Fortier received twelve years in prison for his involvement in the plan.
b. Terry Nichols received life in prison for his role in the Oklahoma City bombing.
c. Tim McVeigh was sentenced to death for this role in the Oklahoma City bombing.
d. Tim McVeigh is still in prison, awaiting the fulfillment of the death sentence he was given.

Vocabulary: *Match each word with its correct definition. Use a dictionary to help if necessary.*

a. catastrophe
b. culprit
c. conspirator

d. infringement
e. arraignment

1._____ one who takes part in a plot or scheme

2._____ to call or bring before a court to answer to an indictment

3._____ a person guilty of an offense or crime

4._____ a violation of

5._____ a sudden disaster

Guided Reading: *Fill in the blanks below to create complete sentences.*

6. By the time the rescue teams had finished, 168 _____ had been reported.

7. Tim McVeigh had been arrested in _____, Oklahoma on an unrelated concealed weapons charge.

8. McVeigh was a US _____ veteran who had served in the Persian Gulf War.

9. McVeigh and Nichols saw the raid against the Branch Davidians as an infringement of _____.

10. Tim McVeigh, Terry _____, and Michael Fortier were all arrested and placed on trial for their involvement in the bombing of the Murrah Federal Building.

Correct the Statement: *Each of the following sentences is false. Circle the incorrect word and write the word or phrase that makes the statement correct in the answer blank provided.*

11. More than 5,000 people were wounded in the Oklahoma City bombing. _____.

12. At first, the investigators suspected the work of European terrorists. _____.

13. It was eventually discovered that the primary culprit was a Canadian named Tim McVeigh. _____.

14. In 1993, federal agents conducted a siege of the compound owned by a religious group known as the Branch Davidians in Dallas, Texas. _____.

15. McVeigh was the first prisoner to be executed by the federal government since 1936. _____.

Summarize: *Answer the following questions in the space provided. Attempt to respond in a complete sentence for each question. Be sure to use correct capitalization and punctuation!*

1. Who was the primary culprit responsible for the Oklahoma City bombing?

2. What was the name of the building which was destroyed?

3. When did the explosion occur?

4. Where was Tim McVeigh arrested?

5. Why did the conspirators choose Oklahoma City as their target?

6. How fast did rescue crews have to work their way through the rubble and why?

Student Response: *Write a paragraph addressing the questions raised below. A thorough response should consist of three to five complete sentences.*

7. Most people who were alive in 1995 can remember where they were when they heard that the Alfred P. Murrah Federal Building had been bombed. If possible, find someone who was alive at the time and interview them. Document their memories below in as much detail as possible. If no one is available, research an eyewitness account online and summarize the main points below.

Unit Five:
Notable Oklahomans

Notable Women in Oklahoma History

There have been many prominent women in the history of Oklahoma. Who are some of these women? What did they do to become memorable?

Kate Barnard was the first woman to be elected as a state official in Oklahoma. She served two four-year terms as the Oklahoma Commissioner of Charities and Corrections. At the time, this was the only elected position that the state constitution allowed a woman to hold. As commissioner, she was a central figure in the passage of compulsory education laws. She also worked to bring an end to child labor and unsafe working conditions.

Kate Barnard

Angie Debo is remembered as Oklahoma's greatest historian. She wrote thirteen books and hundreds of articles over the course of her career, focusing on the history of the state as well as Native American issues. Her book titled *And Still the Waters Run: The Betrayal of the Five Civilized Tribes* was highly controversial at its time of publication. However, this book is remembered today as one of the most influential works on Native American History.

Wilma Mankiller became the first female principal chief of the Cherokee. She held this position from 1985 to 1995. She became principal chief after Ross Swimmer resigned when he was appointed head of the U.S. Bureau of Indian Affairs. Two years later, in 1987, Mankiller was elected to the position outright. In 1991, she won re-election with an astounding 83% of the vote. Mankiller's term in office is usually regarded as a success. She helped revitalize the Cherokee Nation and implemented many programs which were beneficial to the Cherokee people.

Ada Lois Sipuel was a significant figure in the Civil Rights Movement in Oklahoma. In 1946, Sipuel applied for admission into the University of Oklahoma and was denied because she was African American. She took her case to court, and in 1948, the U.S. Supreme Court heard the case *Sipuel v. the Board of Regents of Univ. of Okla.* The Court determined that the state of Oklahoma was required to provide instruction to all students, regardless of race. On June 18, 1949, Sipuel became the first African American to attend the University of Oklahoma's law school. She graduated from the university in 1951 and began practicing law in her hometown of Chickasha.

Another prominent Civil Rights leader was Clara Luper. Luper served as an advisor to the Oklahoma City NAACP Youth Council. She organized sit-ins and other forms of protests in the Oklahoma City area. She worked tirelessly to gain employment rights and voting rights for African Americans. She also fought to achieve integration in restaurants, theaters, and hotels.

> *Words to watch for:*
>
> *compulsory   implemented*
>
> *integration   prodigious*

The Five Moons are five Native American ballerinas from the state of Oklahoma. All five achieved international acclaim for their prodigious talents. This group includes Maria Tallchief, Marjorie Tallchief, Yvonne Chouteau, Rosella Hightower, and Moscelyne Larkin. All five dancers performed for many different dance companies throughout the 20th Century. Yvonne Chouteau established the Oklahoma City Ballet, while Moscelyne Larkin founded the Tulsa Ballet Theatre. They have been honored with a sculpture in Tulsa which is entitled *The Five Moons*.

One of the most notable female entertainers from the state of Oklahoma is Reba McEntire. McEntire has been a standout performer both as a singer and actress. She has produced more than twenty-five albums which led to twenty-five #1 singles as well as fifty-six songs in the Top 10. She has also appeared in seven different films, starred in a popular television series, and even performed on Broadway.

Multiple Choice: *Select the choice that completes the statement or answers the question.*

1._____ Which of the following is Kate Barnard significant for?
a. She became the first female principal chief of a major Native American tribe.
b. She was the first woman appointed to the Oklahoma State Supreme Court.
c. She became the first woman elected as a state official in Oklahoma.
d. She was the first female governor of the state of Oklahoma.

2._____ Which of the following did Wilma Mankiller become well-known for?
a. She was a notorious serial killer who lived in Oklahoma City.
b. She was the first female principal chief of the Cherokee.
c. She was a prominent historian who wrote many books.
d. She was a leader in the Civil Rights Movement throughout the 1960s.

3._____ Which of the following is true of Ada Louis Sipuel?
a. Sipuel became the first African American to register to vote in the state of Oklahoma.
b. Sipuel became a well-known author in the 1960s and sold more than 10 million books.
c. Sipuel became the first woman elected to the House of Representatives for the state of Oklahoma.
d. Sipuel became the first African American to attend the University of Oklahoma's law school.

4._____ Which of the following statements about Clara Luper is inaccurate?
a. Luper served as an adviser to the Oklahoma City NAACP Youth Council.
b. Luper organized sit-ins and other forms of protests in the Oklahoma City area.
c. Luper gained enough recognition that she spoke at the March on Washington in 1963.
d. Luper fought to achieve integration in restaurants, theaters, and hotels.

5._____ Which of the following statements is not true of the Five Moons?
a. All five achieved international fame for their prodigious talents as dancers.
b. All five performed for many different dance companies throughout the 20th Century.
c. All five dancers have established their own ballet studios and theaters.
d. All five have been honored with a sculpture in Tulsa entitled *The Five Moons*.

Vocabulary: *Match each word with its correct definition. Consider how the word is used in the lesson. This might help you define each term. Use a dictionary to help if necessary.*

a. compulsory
b. implement
c. admission
d. integration
e. prodigious

6._____ to put into effect by way of a plan

7._____ required or mandatory

8._____ the act of combining racially divided facilities into unified facilities

9._____ granting permission to enter

10._____ extraordinary in amount; tremendous

Guided Reading: *Fill in the blanks below to create complete sentences.*

1. As Commissioner of Charities and Corrections, Kate Barnard was a central figure in the passage of compulsory _____ laws.

2. In 1991, Wilma Mankiller won re-election with an astounding _____ of the vote.

3. The Supreme Court determined that the state of Oklahoma was required to provide instruction to all students, regardless of _____.

4. The Five Moons include _____, Marjorie Tallchief, Yvonne Chouteau, Rosella Hightower, and Moscelyne Larkin.

5. Reba McEntire has produced more than _____ albums which led to twenty-five #1 singles.

Matching: *Match the notable Oklahoma woman with one of her significant accomplishments:*

a. Kate Barnard
b. Angie Debo
c. Wilma Mankiller

d. Ada Louis Sipuel
e. Clara Luper

6._____ helped revitalize the Cherokee Nation and implemented programs beneficial to the tribe

7._____ became the first African American to attend the University of Oklahoma's law school

8._____ worked tirelessly to gain employment rights and voting rights for African Americans

9._____ worked to bring an end to child labor and unsafe working conditions

10._____ wrote thirteen books and hundreds of articles focusing on the history of Oklahoma

Summarize: *Answer the following questions in the space provided. Attempt to respond in a complete sentence for each question. Be sure to use correct capitalization and punctuation!*

1. Who is remembered as Oklahoma's greatest historian?

2. What is the title of Angie Debo's most well-known book?

3. When did Wilma Mankiller hold office?

4. Where did Reba McEntire perform other than in movies and television shows?

5. Why could Kate Barnard only serve as the Commissioner of Charities and Corrections?

6. How did Clara Luper work to achieve civil rights? (what were some of the events she organized?)

Student Response: *Write a paragraph addressing the questions raised below. A thorough response should consist of three to five complete sentences.*

7. Of the women mentioned in this lesson, which do you feel made the most significant contribution to the state of Oklahoma? Explain your answer, citing specific textual evidence.

Notable Oklahoma Governors

Oklahoma has had several notable governors throughout the years, both good and bad. Who were some of these governors? What did they do that was noteworthy?

Governor E.W. Marland was the 10th governor of Oklahoma. He was elected to the position following the term of William H. Murray. Marland was an incredibly successful businessman and founder of the Marland Oil Company (which later became Conoco). At one point, Marland was worth more than $85 million. As governor, he attempted to implement the "Little Deal" program to coincide with President Franklin Roosevelt's "New Deal" program. This was a relief program designed to aid struggling families during the tough years of the Great Depression. Unfortunately, a stubborn state legislature refused to pass many of his proposals.

Robert S. Kerr was elected in 1942 to become the state's 12th governor. Kerr had become prosperous in the oil industry with a company known as the Anderson-Kerr Drilling Company (later known as Kerr-McGee). He became the first governor who was actually born in Oklahoma. As governor, he brought many wartime industries to the state, as well as military training sites. He gained enough notoriety as governor that he was selected as the keynote speaker at the 1944 Democrat National Convention. Following his term as governor, he served as a United States senator for Oklahoma from 1949 to 1963.

Oklahoma's 15th governor was elected in 1954. Raymond Gary assumed the office at a critical time in the nation's history. He oversaw the first steps of Oklahoma's desegregation process at the end of the Jim Crow era. One of his first actions as governor was ordering that the "whites only" and "colored only" signs be removed from the restrooms at the state capital building. In a statewide radio address, he announced that defiance to the Supreme Court decision of *Brown v. the Board of Education* would not be tolerated. He stated that school districts that refused to integrate would find themselves on their own.

George Nigh was both the 17th and 22nd governor of Oklahoma. He briefly served as governor in January of 1963, after Howard Edmondson resigned (Nigh was lieutenant governor at the time). This brief stint as governor only lasted eight days! However, Nigh returned to the office in 1979. By winning re-election in 1982, he became Oklahoma's first two term governor. All previous governors had been limited by law to one term.

Henry Bellmon became Oklahoma's first Republican governor. He was elected in 1962 as the state's 18th governor. Following his term as governor, he served as the chairman for Richard Nixon's presidential campaign in 1968. He also served two terms as a United States senator from 1969 through 1981. In 1986, he was elected to the governor's office again as the state's 23rd governor. During his second term in office, he and the state legislature worked to pass House Bill 1017. This was a major piece of education reform which provided additional funding for schools.

> *Words to watch for:*
>
> *coincide   notoriety*
>
> *defiance   indicted*

Oklahoma's 20th governor was David Hall. While in office, Hall passed the Oklahoma Income Tax Act, establishing the state's income tax. Shortly after leaving office in 1975, he was indicted on charges of racketeering, extortion, and bribery. He became Oklahoma's first governor to be convicted of criminal charges for illegal activities that took place while he was in office. He eventually served 19 months in a federal prison.

Mary Fallin was elected as Oklahoma's 27th governor in 2010. She became the first female governor in the state's history. Prior to assuming the role of governor, she was a member of the U.S. House of Representatives and served as the state's lieutenant governor for twelve years.

Multiple Choice: *Select the choice that completes the statement or answers the question.*

1._____ Which of the following best describes the "Little Deal" program implemented by E.W. Marland?
a. a program designed to benefit struggling school districts and provide funds for education
b. a weekly radio program in which the governor would address the people of the state
c. a relief program designed to aid struggling families during the Great Depression
d. a popular radio game show in which the governor would give away prizes to families

2._____ Which of the following statements about Robert S. Kerr is probably *most* significant?
a. Kerr was the first governor who was actually born in Oklahoma.
b. Kerr brought wartime industries and military training sites to the state.
c. Kerr was the keynote speaker at the 1944 Democrat National Convention.
d. Kerr served as a U.S. senator from 1949 to 1963.

3._____ Which of the following events did Raymond Gary oversee while he was governor?
a. He oversaw the aftermath of the Oklahoma City bombing.
b. He oversaw anti-war protests during the turbulent decade of the 1960s.
c. He oversaw a dramatic restructuring of the state's government and tax code.
d. He oversaw Oklahoma's desegregation process at the end of the Jim Crow era.

4._____ Henry Bellmon has which of the following distinctions?
a. He was Oklahoma's first Republican governor.
b. He was the first Oklahoma governor to be removed from office.
c. He was the first governor to be elected to a second term.
d. He was Oklahoma's first governor.

5._____ Which of the following did David Hall become best remembered for?
a. He became the first governor to seek a third term and won a narrow election against his Republican challenger.
b. He became the first governor convicted of criminal charges for illegal activities which occurred while he was in office.
c. He became the first governor to declare martial law, which he did as they were attempting to remove him from office.
d. He became the last governor to be elected by the legislature. All governors are now elected by popular vote.

Vocabulary: *Match each word with its correct definition. Consider how the word is used in the lesson. This might help you define each term. Use a dictionary to help if necessary.*

a. coincide
b. notoriety
c. keynote

d. defiance
e. indict

6._____ the main idea; central program; most important part

7._____ to occur at exactly the same time

8._____ to bring a formal accusation against

9._____ bold resistance to authority

10._____ celebrated; well-known

Guided Reading: *Fill in the blanks below to create complete sentences.*

1. Marland was an incredibly successful businessman and founder of the Marland Oil Company (which later became _____).

2. At one point, Marland was worth more than $_____.

3. Kerr had become prosperous in the oil industry with a company known as the Anderson-Kerr Drilling Company (later known as _____).

4. Robert S. Kerr became the first governor who was actually _____ in Oklahoma.

5. One of Raymond Gary's first actions as governor was ordering that the "whites only" and "colored only" signs be removed from the _____ at the state capital building.

6. Governor Gary stated that school districts that refused to _____ would find themselves on their own.

7. Henry Bellmon also served two terms as a United States _____ from 1969 through 1981.

8. George Nigh became Oklahoma's first _____ governor.

9. While in office, David Hall passed the Oklahoma _____ Act.

10. Mary Fallin became the first _____ governor in the state's history.

Summarize: *Answer the following questions in the space provided. Attempt to respond in a complete sentence for each question. Be sure to use correct capitalization and punctuation!*

1. Who was Oklahoma's first female governor?

2. What position did Henry Bellmon hold in 1968?

3. When did Robert S. Kerr speak at the Democratic National Convention?

4. Where did David Hall have to go after his term as governor was over?

5. Why were many of the "Little Deal" proposals not passed?

6. How long was George Nigh governor the first time he held the office?

Student Response: *Write a paragraph addressing the questions raised below. A thorough response should consist of three to five complete sentences.*

7. Would you like to be the governor of Oklahoma? Why or why not? Explain your answer.

Notable Oklahoma Artists

There are several artists from Oklahoma who have become well-known. Who are these artists? What are they known for?

Spencer Asah, James Auchiah, Jack Hokeah, Stephen Mopope, Lois Smoky, and Monroe Tsatoke create the group known as the Kiowa Six. All of these artists were born in Oklahoma in the early 1900s near the Anadarko area. Five of them attended the St. Patrick's Mission School. This was a school in Anadarko which served Kiowa, Comanche, and Apache children. They received their artistic training from a Choctaw nun, Sister Mary Olivia Taylor.

The Kiowa Six became influential painters throughout the 1920s. They were well-known for their paintings of tribal dancers, ceremonies, and Kiowa daily life. Their careers became an inspiration for future generations of Native American artists.

> *Words to watch for:*
>
> *prolific   influential*
>
> *grotesque   accolades*

Jerome Tiger was a prolific Native American artist from Tahlequah, Oklahoma. The art world was introduced to Tiger in 1961. Over the next six years, he produced hundreds of paintings.

Unfortunately, his life was tragically cut short. He died in 1967 at the age of 26. His paintings can still be seen today at the Philbrook Museum of Art as well as the Gilcrease Museum, both in Tulsa. He also has paintings in the Five Civilized Tribes Museum in Muskogee and the Woolaroc Museum in Bartlesville.

Chester Gould was born in Pawnee, Oklahoma. On October, 4th, 1931, Gould introduced newspaper readers to a comic strip hero named Dick Tracy. Tracy was a daring detective who battled an endless string of villains, some of which were grotesque or bizarre in appearance. Throughout his career, Gould won many different accolades for his comic strip, and his drawings have even been displayed in museums. In fact, there was even a Chester Gould-Dick Tracy Museum in Woodstock, Illinois!

Gould continued drawing *Dick Tracy* until December 25, 1977. He died in 1985 of congestive heart failure, but the memory of his work lives on. *Dick Tracy* is still printed in newspapers across the country, and the character has appeared in his own radio show, cartoon show, live-action television series, and even a major motion picture.

Multiple Choice: *Select the choice that completes the statement or answers the question.*

1._____ Which of the following is *not* true of the Kiowa Six?
a. All of the artists were born in Oklahoma in the early 1900s, near Anadarko.
b. All six of them attended St. Patrick's Mission School.
c. Most of them received their artistic training from Sister Maria Olivia Taylor.
d. The Kiowa Six became prominent painters throughout the 1920s.

2._____ The Kiowa Six became well-known for which types of work?
a. They sculpted statues in the shapes of animals native to North America.
b. They painted scenes of beautiful places they had never visited.
c. They painted abstract images that were evoked after long hours of meditation.
d. They painted tribal dancers, ceremonies, and Kiowa daily life.

3._____ Which of the following best summarizes the career of Jerome Tiger?
a. He had a brief career in which he produced hundreds of paintings, before dying at a young age.
b. He had a very long career, producing thousands of works and dying as an old man.
c. He did not start painting until very late in his life and became famous when he was in his 70s.
d. He was a child prodigy who became a famous artist before he was a teenager. He continued painting throughout his life.

4._____ Which of the following locations is not mentioned as displaying artwork by Jerome Tiger?
a. The Philbrook Museum of Art   c. The Oklahoma Historical Center
b. The Gilcrease Museum   d. The Woolaroc Museum

5._____ Which of the following best describes the character of Dick Tracy?
a. Tracy was a wise-cracking teenager with an imaginary best friend.
b. Tracy was a daring detective who battled an unending string of villains.
c. Tracy was a mischievous rabbit who enjoyed playing tricks on people.
d. Tracy was a bumbling husband whose wife was always getting mad at him.

Vocabulary: *Match each word with its correct definition. Consider how the word is used in the lesson. This might help you define each term. Use a dictionary to help if necessary.*

a. prolific   d. grotesque
b. influential   e. accolades
c. tragic

6._____ shocking or sad

7._____ unnatural in shape or appearance

8._____ producing large quantities

9._____ someone or something that has a major impact on others

10._____ high praise, awards, or honors

Guided Reading: *Fill in the blanks below to create complete sentences.*

1. _____, James Auchiah, Jack Hokeah, Stephen Mopope, Lois Smoky, and Monroe Tsatoke created the group known as the Kiowa Six.

2. All of these artists were born in Oklahoma in the early 1900s, near the _____ area.

3. The St. Patrick Mission School served _____, Comanche, and Apache children.

4. The careers of the Kiowa Six became an inspiration for future generations of Native American _____.

5. Jerome Tiger was a prolific Native American artist from _____, Oklahoma.

Correct the Statement: *Each of the following sentences is false. Circle the incorrect word(s) and write the word or phrase that makes the statement correct in the answer blank provided.*

6. Jerome Tiger died in 1967 at the age of 66. _____.

7. Tiger's sculptures can still be seen today at the Philbrook Museum of Art as well as the Gilcrease Museum, both in Tulsa. _____.

8. On October, 4th, 1931, Gould introduced television audiences to a comic strip hero hero known as Dick Tracy. _____.

9. Chester Gould died in 1995 of congestive heart failure. _____.

10. Dick Tracy is no longer printed in newspapers across the country. _____.

Summarize: *Answer the following questions in the space provided. Attempt to respond in a complete sentence for each question. Be sure to use correct capitalization and punctuation.*

1. Who created the character Dick Tracy?

2. What did the Kiowa Six paint images of?

3. When did *Dick Tracy* first appear in newspapers?

4. Where did the Kiowa Six attend school?

5. Why did Jerome Tiger's career come to an unexpected end?

6. How has the character of Dick Tracy lived on?

Student Response: *Write a paragraph addressing the questions raised below. A thorough response should consist of three to five complete sentences.*

7. Using an outside source, find an image painted by one of the Kiowa Six, Jerome Tiger, or an illustration by Chester Gould and draw your own version of this image in the space provided.

Notable Oklahoma Authors

Oklahoma has produced several well-known authors throughout its history. Who are these authors? What books are they known for?

In 1952, Ralph Ellison published his controversial novel _Invisible Man._ The narrator of the story is thought of as "invisible" because people refuse to see him. The book explores the topic of racism and how Northern racism differed from Southern racism. Ellison was awarded the National Book Award for Fiction in 1953. Despite this early success, Ellison did not publish another book in his lifetime. His second novel, _Juneteenth_, was published posthumously, five years after his death. However, he continued writing poetry and articles about his experiences as an African American. Amongst his poetry, he wrote a tribute to the Deep Deuce district of Oklahoma City where he was raised. This was a district of Oklahoma City which became a regional center for African American music, culture, and commerce. Ellison received the Presidential Medal of Freedom in 1969. Following his death in 1994, many of his unpublished manuscripts became available to the public.

N. Scott Momaday is a Native American author and member of the Kiowa Tribe. He won the Pulitzer Prize for Fiction in 1969 for his novel _House Made of Dawn_. It is widely thought of as the novel that led to Native American fiction being accepted in the mainstream culture. The novel tells the story of a young Native American returning to the reservation after fighting in World War II. To this day, it is thought of as a classic of Native American literature.

Words to watch for:
author   posthumously
manuscripts   conveys

Raised in Chickasha, Oklahoma, Bill Wallace graduated from the University of Oklahoma. He worked as a 4th Grade teacher and a principal before becoming successful as an author. He eventually wrote thirty-one books. Amongst his more well-known titles are _A Dog Called Kitty_ and _Trapped in Death Cave_. He has won numerous awards for his writing, including the Sequoyah Children's Book Award.

Rifles For Watie was not the first book that Harold Keith published, but it is certainly the one he is best remembered for. _Rifles for Watie_ conveys the story of a sixteen-year-old boy who gets caught up in the Civil War. The novel won the Newbery Medal in 1958. This is an award which is given to the best children's book of the year. Keith would eventually go on to publish 15 books on a variety of topics.

S.E. Hinton became a well-known author while she was still a teenager. Her first novel, _The Outsiders_, was published in 1967 when she was only eighteen and a freshman in college. _The Outsiders_ is a coming-of-age tale that explores the world of teenagers in 1960s Oklahoma. The novel has sold more than 14 million copies and continues to sell thousands each year. It was even made into a major motion picture in 1983, starring Tom Cruise, Emilio Estevez, and Patrick Swayze. Hinton's other novels include _That was Then... This is Now_, _Rumble Fish_, and several others.

Multiple Choice: *Select the choice that completes the statement or answers the question.*

1._____ Which of the following best describes Ralph Ellison's novel *Invisible Man*?
a. The novel is about a science experiment which leaves the scientist invisible.
b. The novel explores how Northern racism is different than Southern racism.
c. The novel is about the inner workings of politics and what goes on behind the scenes.
d. The novel explores the misery of a man whose love interest has replaced him with another.

2._____ Which of the following best explains the significance of the Deep Deuce District?
a. This was a district in Oklahoma City that became well-known for producing talented athletes.
b. This was a district in Oklahoma City that became legendary for its restaurants.
c. This was a district in Oklahoma City that produced many of the state's future political leaders.
d. This was a district in Oklahoma City that was well-known for African American music, culture, and commerce.

3._____ Which of the following best explains the significance of *House Made of Dawn*?
a. The novel was written by N. Scott Momaday, a member of the Kiowa tribe.
b. The novel tells the story of a Native American returning to the reservation after fighting in World War II.
c. It is viewed as the novel that led to Native American fiction being accepted by mainstream culture.
d. N. Scott Momaday won the Pulitzer Prize for Fiction in 1969.

4._____ Which of the following statements about Bill Wallace's life is inaccurate?
a. Wallace worked as a 4th Grade teacher and a principal before becoming an author.
b. Wallace eventually wrote more than thirty-one books in his life.
c. Wallace's most well-known books are *A Dog Called Kitty* and *Trapped in Death Cave*.
d. Wallace has won numerous awards, including the Newbery Medal.

5._____ Which of the following best describes S.E. Hinton's novel *The Outsiders*?
a. *The Outsiders* is a science-fiction novel about visitors from another planet.
b. *The Outsiders* is a coming of age story about teenagers living in Oklahoma.
c. *The Outsiders* is about a group of hill people who come in contact with the civilized world.
d. *The Outsiders* is a fantasy story about tiny people who live in the forest.

Vocabulary: *Match each word with its correct definition. Consider how the word is used in the lesson. This might help you define each term. Use a dictionary to help if necessary.*

a. author
b. narrator
c. posthumous
d. manuscript
e. convey

6._____ a person who writes novels, poems, or essays; a writer

7._____ occurring after death

8._____ the original text of an author's work; an unpublished book

9._____ to communicate; relay

10._____ the person who tells the story of events

Guided Reading: *Fill in the blanks below to create complete sentences.*

1. Ellison was awarded the National Book Award for _____ in 1953.

2. To this day, *House Made of Dawn* it is thought of as a _____ of Native American literature.

3. Raised in _____, Oklahoma, Bill Wallace graduated from the University of Oklahoma.

4. *Rifles for Watie* conveys the story of a sixteen-year-old boy who gets caught up in the _____.

5. S.E. Hinton became a well-known author while she was still a _____.

Matching: *Match the Oklahoma author with the title of their most famous work:*

a. Ralph Ellison
b. N. Scott Momaday
c. Bill Wallace

d. Harold Keith
e. S.E. Hinton

6._____*Rifles for Watie*

7._____*Insvisible Man*

8._____*A Dog Called Kitty*

9._____*House Made of Dawn*

10._____ *The Outsiders*

Summarize: *Answer the following questions in the space provided. Attempt to respond in a complete sentence for each question. Be sure to use correct capitalization and punctuation!*

1. Who starred in the film version of *The Outsiders*?

2. What story does *House Made of Dawn* tell?

3. When did Harold Keith win the Newbery Medal?

4. Where was Ralph Ellison raised?

5. Why was the Deep Deuce district significant?

6. How many copies has *The Outsiders* sold?

Student Response: *Write a paragraph addressing the questions raised below. A thorough response should consist of three to five complete sentences.*

7. Have you read any of the books mentioned in this lesson? If so, which one? Relay what you remember about the plot. If not, which one sounds the most interesting to you and why? Explain your answer as thoroughly as possible.

Notable Oklahoma Athletes

Jim Thorpe isn't the only famous athlete to come from the state of Oklahoma. Who are some of these other famous athletes? What sports did they participate in?

Allie P. Reynolds came from Bethany, Oklahoma. A member of the Creek Nation, Reynolds attended Oklahoma A&M where he excelled at both baseball and football. Reynolds had a twelve year baseball career, pitching for both the Cleveland Indians and the New York Yankees. Nicknamed "Superchief", Reynolds compiled 182 wins and over 1,400 strikeouts. He was a six time all-star and played on six World Series championship teams.

1951 was the rookie season for Mickey Mantle. It was the beginning of a legendary eighteen year baseball career. Mantle played centerfield and 1st base for the New York Yankees. He hit 536 homeruns in his career, was a sixteen time all-star, and won the American League Most Valuable Player award three times. He played in twelve World Series, winning seven of them. He also holds the record for most World Series homeruns with 18. Mantle was inducted into the Baseball Hall of Fame in 1974 and is remembered today as one of the greatest to ever play the game.

As Mantle's career with the Yankees was coming to a close, Bobby Murcer's was just beginning. Murcer played baseball for seventeen seasons, playing in the outfield for the Yankees, the San Francisco Giants, and the Chicago Cubs. Murcer was a five time all-star and won a Gold Glove in 1972. Murcer returned to the Yankees as a broadcaster from 1983 to 1998.

Words to watch for:

excelled   compiled

decorated   competition

Johnny Bench, from Binger, Oklahoma, played catcher for the Cincinnati Reds from 1967 to 1983. He was selected the National League Most Valuable Player twice and won two World Series. He was selected to fourteen all-star games and his #5 was retired by the Reds. He won ten Gold Gloves at his position and is thought by most to be the greatest catcher to ever play baseball. In 1989, he was inducted into the Baseball Hall of Fame, garnering 96% of the votes.

Steve Largent was an All-American wide receiver at the University of Tulsa. He played thirteen seasons with the Seattle Seahawks where he became one of the greatest receivers to ever play football. He was selected to the Pro Bowl seven times and, at the time of his retirement, held the NFL records for most receptions in a career, most receiving yards, and most touchdown receptions. He was elected into the Pro Football Hall of Fame in 1995.

Mark Price is one of Oklahoma's most successful basketball players. Raised in Enid, Oklahoma, Price became a standout at Georgia Tech University. He played point guard in the NBA for twelve seasons, playing most of his career with the Cleveland Cavaliers. Price was selected as an NBA all-star four times and won the annual three-point shootout twice. He finished his NBA career with more than 10,000 points and over 4,800 assists. His #25 is one of only seven that has been retired by the Cleveland Cavaliers.

Troy Aikman, from Henryetta, Oklahoma, was the first pick in the 1989 NFL draft. He played quarterback for the Dallas Cowboys for twelve seasons, accumulating nearly 33,000 passing yards and 165 touchdown passes. He was selected to the Pro Bowl six times and won three Super Bowls. Aikman was elected to the Pro Football Hall of Fame in 2006. He is also a member of the College Football Hall of Fame and the Dallas Cowboy Ring of Honor.

Shannon Miller was raised in Edmond, Oklahoma. She burst onto the world gymnastics scene in 1992 at the Summer Olympic Games in Barcelona, Spain. She won two silver medals in 1992, for the balance beam and the all-around competition. She also received three bronze medals for the uneven bars and floor exercise, as well as the team competition. Four years later, she competed again in the Summer Olympics in Atlanta, Georgia. She won the gold medal for the balance beam and also received a gold as part of the team competition. Throughout the 1990s, Miller also won nine medals in World Championship competition. She is the most highly-decorated American gymnast, male or female, in history.

There are many other successful athletes from the state of Oklahoma. Joe Carter, Tommy Morrison, Bart Conner, and Blake Griffin are just a few of the sports stars who have called Oklahoma home. The state will surely continue to produce many fine athletes as the years go by.

Multiple Choice: *Select the choice that completes the statement or answers the question.*

1._____ Which of the following best describes Mickey Mantle's playing career?
a.   He played for the New York Yankees and is remembered today as one of the greatest to ever play baseball.
b.   He played baseball for the New York Mets and was elected to the Hall of Fame in 1974.
c.   He was a standout wide receiver for Seattle Seahawks and became one of the greatest receivers in NFL history.
d.   He was a successful quarterback in college, but became a running back when he transitioned to the NFL.

2._____ Which of the following is not true of Johnny Bench's career?
a.   Bench was selected to fourteen all-star games.
b.   Bench's #5 is worn by every catcher in the league today.
c.   Bench is thought by most to be the greatest catcher to ever play the game.
d.   Bench was elected to the Hall of Fame in 1989 with 96% of the vote.

3._____ Which of the following statements about Steve Largent is inaccurate?
a.   Largent played thirteen seasons with the Seattle Super Sonics.
b.   Largent was elected to the Pro Bowl seven times.
c.   Largent held the NFL record for most receiving yards at the time of his retirement.
d.   Largent was elected to the Pro Football Hall of Fame in 1995.

4._____ Which of the following best summarizes Mark Price's playing career?
a.   Price was a quarterback for the Cleveland Browns, accumulating more than 33,000 passing yards.
b.   Price was a pitcher for the Cleveland Indians, striking out more than 3,000 batters in his long career.
c.   Price was a power forward for the Cleveland Cavaliers, scoring more than 15,000 points in his career.
d.   Price was a point guard for the Cleveland Cavaliers, eventually having his number retired.

5._____ Which of the following feats did Shannon Miller not accomplish?
a.   She won two silver and three bronze medals at the 1992 Summer Olympics.
b.   She became the first female gymnast to win gold medals on all four events.
c.   She won two gold medals at the 1996 Summer Olympics in Atlanta, Georgia.
d.   She won nine medals in World Championship competition throughout the 1990s.

Vocabulary: *Match each word with its correct definition. Consider how the word is used in the lesson. This might help you define each term. Use a dictionary to help if necessary.*

a. excel
b. compile
c. garner
d. decorated
e. competition

6._____ to gather or collect

7._____ to put together into one unit

8._____ a contest, usually for some sort of prize

9._____ having received many awards

10._____ to surpass others in quality of performance

Name_____

Guided Reading: *Fill in the blanks below to create complete sentences.*

1. Mickey Mantle hit _____ homeruns in his career.

2. Johnny Bench was selected the National League _____ twice and won two World Series.

3. Steve Largent became one of the greatest _____ to ever play football.

4. Troy Aikman was selected to the Pro Bowl six times and won three _____.

5. Joe Carter, Tommy Morrison, _____, and Blake Griffin are just a few of the sports stars who have called Oklahoma home.

Matching: *Match the Oklahoma athlete with the correct professional team each played for:*

a. New York Yankees   d. Cleveland Cavaliers
b. Cincinnati Reds   e. Dallas Cowboys
c. Seattle Seahawks

6._____ Troy Aikman

7._____ Steve Largent

8._____ Mickey Mantle

9._____ Mark Price

10._____ Johnny Bench

Summarize: *Answer the following questions in the space provided. Attempt to respond in a complete sentence for each question. Be sure to use correct capitalization and punctuation!*

1. Who became the Yankees broadcaster from 1983 to 1998?

2. What was Allie P. Reynolds' nickname?

3. When did Shannon Miller win her gold medals at the Olympics?

4. Where did Steve Largent play college football?

5. Why do you suppose Troy Aikman is in the Dallas Cowboy Ring of Honor? (Which of his feats probably led to this inclusion?)

6. How is Mickey Mantle remembered today?

Student Response: *Write a paragraph addressing the questions raised below. A thorough response should consist of three to five complete sentences.*

7. There are several athletes mentioned in the final paragraph of this lesson. Pick one of these athletes that you are unfamiliar with and, using an outside source, write a brief biography of this athlete's accomplishments.

Notable Oklahoma Country & Western Musicians

Country & Western music has long been a part of the state of Oklahoma. Who are some of the prominent singers from the state? What songs are they known for?

One of the earliest country performers to call Oklahoma home was Bob Wills. While Wills was not born in Oklahoma, he moved to the state in 1934 with his group the Texas Playboys. Bob Wills and the Texas Playboys began performing on an Oklahoma City radio station, KVOO, on a noontime show, Monday through Friday. By 1940, the Texas Playboys were popular nationwide. Their song "New San Antonio Rose" sold a million records and became their signature song. Wills became an inspiration to countless performers who followed him.

Wanda Jackson was born in Maud, Oklahoma and lived much of her life in Oklahoma City. Jackson had an extremely successful music career throughout the late 1950s and 1960s. Her hit songs span several genres from rock, to country, rockabilly, and gospel. She is thought of as the "Queen of Rockabilly" and in 2009, she was inducted into the Rock n' Roll Hall of Fame. She has also been listed as one of the 40 Greatest Women in Country Music.

Wanda Jackson

Roger Miller was born in Fort Worth, Texas, but moved to Erick, Oklahoma at a young age. He started performing in the 1950s and signed his first recording contract in 1958. He had three #1 songs including the incredibly popular "King of the Road". Miller won eleven Grammy Awards and was inducted into the Country Music Hall of Fame in 1995.

In 1989, Garth Brooks, from Yukon, Oklahoma, redefined country music. Throughout the 1990s, he produced a string of hit songs unmatched by virtually any performer in the history of popular music. Brooks became a pop culture phenomenon with television specials and even fashion trends. Brooks was awarded "Entertainer of the Year" four times in a row by the Country Music Association. Throughout his career, he recorded eighteen #1 songs and sold millions of albums. His most popular songs include "Friends in Low Places", "The Thunder Rolls", and "The Dance".

> *Words to watch for:*
>
> *signature   inducted*
>
> *phenomenon   virtually*

Toby Keith, born in Clinton and raised in Moore, Oklahoma, released his debut album in 1993. His debut single, "Should've Been a Cowboy" became a #1 hit and remains his signature song. This was the beginning of an impressive career that has included twenty #1 singles and more than fifteen studio albums. *Billboard* named Keith the Country Music Artist of the Decade for the decade of the 2000s.

There have been many other Country & Western performers who have come from the state of Oklahoma. Vince Gill, Reba McEntire, Ronnie Dunn, Joe Diffie, and Carrie Underwood are just a few of the many country singers who have called the state home.

Multiple Choice: *Select the choice that completes the statement or answers the question.*

1._____ Which of the following pieces of information about Bob Wills is most significant?
a. Bob Wills moved to Oklahoma in 1934.
b. Bob Wills & The Texas Playboys performed on the Oklahoma City radio station KVOO.
c. Bob Wills' song, "The New San Antonio Rose" sold a million records.
d. Bob Wills became an inspiration to countless performers who followed him.

2._____ Which of the following statements about Wanda Jackson is not accurate?
a. Wanda Jackson won eleven Grammy awards and was nominated for five others.
b. Wanda Jackson is known as the "Queen of Rockabilly."
c. Wanda Jackson was inducted into the Rock n' Roll Hall of Fame.
d. Wanda Jackson has been listed amongst the 40 Greatest Women in Country Music.

3._____ Which of the following best summarizes Roger Miller's career?
a. Miller had three #1 songs, won eleven Grammies, and was inducted into the Country Music Hall of Fame.
b. Miller had brief success performing with other groups, but could never succeed as a solo artist.
c. Miller experienced success in three different decades, becoming one of the most legendary performers of all time.
d. Miller's skill as a musician has gained him greater fame than his solo singing efforts.

4._____ Which of the following statements about Garth Brooks is not true?
a. Brooks was awarded "Entertainer of the Year" four times in a row by the Country Music Association.
b. Brooks recorded 18 #1 songs and sold millions of albums.
c. Brooks was declared the "Greatest Country Performer of All Time" by Rolling Stone Magazine.
d. Brooks' most popular songs include "Friends in Low Places", "The Thunder Rolls", and "The Dance".

5._____ Which of the following statements is not true of Toby Keith's life?
a. Keith released his debut album in 1980.
b. Keith's debut single, "I Should Have Been a Cowboy" became a #1 hit.
c. Keith has recorded at least twenty #1 songs and fifteen studio albums.
d. Keith was named "Country Music Artist of the Decade" for the 2000s.

Vocabulary: *Match each word with its correct definition. Consider how the word is used in the lesson. This might help you define each term. Use a dictionary to help if necessary.*

a. signature
b. inspiration
c. induct
d. phenomenon
e. virtually

6._____ a distinguishing mark or feature that a person is identified with

7._____ for the most part; almost completely

8._____ a remarkable or exceptional occurrence

9._____ a stimulation of the mind; an influence

10._____ to install into an office or position

Guided Reading: *Fill in the blanks below to create complete sentences.*

1. Bob Wills and the _____ began performing on an Oklahoma City radio station, KVOO.

2. Wanda Jackson's hit songs span several genres from rock, to country, rockabilly, and _____.

3. Roger Miller was born in Fort Worth, Texas, but moved to _____, Oklahoma at a young age.

4. Brooks became a pop culture phenomenon with television specials and even _____ trends.

5. _____, Ronnie Dunn, Joe Diffie, and Carrie Underwood are just a few of the many country singers who have called the state home.

Matching: *Correctly match each performer with their hometown, or the city in which they became famous.*

a. Bob Wills   d. Garth Brooks
b. Wanda Jackson   e. Toby Keith
c. Roger Miller

6._____ Maud, Oklahoma

7._____ Moore, Oklahoma

8._____ Oklahoma City, Oklahoma

9._____ Erick, Oklahoma

10._____ Yukon, Oklahoma

Name_____

Summarize: *Answer the following questions in the space provided. Attempt to respond in a complete sentence for each question. Be sure to use correct capitalization and punctuation!*

1. Who was named Country Music Artist of the Decade for the 2000s?

2. What was Roger Miller's most successful song?

3. When was Garth Brooks popular?

4. Where did Wanda Jackson live much of her life?

5. Why was Bob Wills significant?

6. How many performers have had the success that Garth Brooks experienced?

Student Response: *Write a paragraph addressing the questions raised below. A thorough response should consist of three to five complete sentences.*

7. Have you heard any of the songs mentioned in this lesson? If so, which ones? Who do you feel is the most prominent musician from the state today?

Other Notables

Oklahoma has produced some other notable politicians and university presidents over the years. Who are some of these individuals? What did they do to become so well-known?

In 1928, Henry G. Bennett became the president of Oklahoma Agricultural & Mechanical College (Oklahoma A&M was later renamed Oklahoma State University). He served in this position from 1928 to 1950.

> *Words to watch for:*
>
> *architectural   turbulent*
>
> *tumultuous   unprecedented*

During his tenure, the university experienced considerable expansion of its facilities. He established a plan that was followed for more than fifty years and helped make the university what it has become today. The architectural style seen on campus today is still a reflection of the work he began during his time as president. Mr. Bennett is honored today with a statue on OSU's main campus in Stillwater, Oklahoma.

George Lynn Cross became the president of Oklahoma University in 1943. He served in this position until 1968. Cross oversaw a period of tremendous growth for the university as enrollment skyrocketed during the post-World War II era. Thirty-seven new buildings were constructed on campus while Cross was president. Cross also presided over the school during the turbulent years of the 1960s when large number of students were protesting American involvement in the Vietnam Conflict. African American integration also occurred during his time as president. Cross is famously quoted as saying that he hoped to "build a university which the football team could be proud of."

Carl Albert

Carl Albert was a member of the House of Representatives for thirty years. During that time, he rose through the political ranks, holding virtually every position of leadership imaginable. He served as both the House Majority Whip and the House Majority Leader at different times in his career. Finally, in 1971, Albert became Speaker of the House. This is the highest political office held by anyone from the state of Oklahoma. He was Speaker of the House during the tumultuous events of 1974 when Richard Nixon resigned the presidency due to the Watergate scandal. Albert retired from politics in 1977 and returned to his home in McAlester.

David Boren was a constant presence in Oklahoma politics throughout the latter half of the 20th Century. From 1975 to 1979, Boren served as Oklahoma's 21st governor. During his time as governor, he reduced the state income tax and eliminated more than a hundred government agencies. In 1978, he decided not to run for a second term as governor and instead ran for a seat in the United States Senate. He represented Oklahoma in the Senate from 1979 through 1994. Following his retirement from the Senate, he became the president of Oklahoma University. The university experienced nearly unprecedented growth and financial success during his time in office.

Multiple Choice: *Select the choice that completes the statement or answers the question.*

1._____ Which of the following best describes Henry G. Bennett's term as president of Oklahoma A&M?
a. The university experienced considerable expansion of its facilities during his tenure.
b. The university underwent African American integration during his tenure.
c. The university experienced a tremendous surge in students from overseas during his tenure.
d. The university underwent a dramatic shift in focus and purpose during his tenure.

2._____ Which of the following statements is inaccurate of George Lynn Cross's tenure at the University of Oklahoma?
a. Thirty-seven new buildings were constructed while he was president.
b. The enrollment skyrocketed during the post-World War I years.
c. Cross oversaw the turbulent years of students protesting the Vietnam Conflict.
d. African American integration occurred during Cross's tenure as president.

3._____ Which of the following facts is probably most significant about the career of Carl Albert?
a. Albert was a member of the House of Representatives for over thirty years.
b. Albert held many different positions of leadership while in office.
c. Albert was House Majority Whip and House Majority Leader at different times.
d. Albert became the Speaker of the House in 1971.

4._____ Carl Albert was Speaker of the House during which of the following events?
a. the assassination of John F. Kennedy
b. the Watergate scandal
c. the Iran-Contra hearings
d. the impeachment of Bill Clinton

5._____ Which of the following did David Boren *not* accomplish?
a. He was Oklahoma's 21st Governor.
b. He represented Oklahoma in the United States Senate.
c. He started a successful multi-billion dollar business.
d. He became the president of the University of Oklahoma.

Vocabulary: *Match each word with its correct definition. Consider how the word is used in the lesson. This might help you define each term. Use a dictionary to help if necessary.*

a. tenure   d. tumultuous
b. architectural   e. unprecedented
c. turbulent

6._____ highly agitated; distraught; full of emotional upheaval

7._____ the period of time someone is in a position

8._____ without previous instance; never been done before

9._____ the physical characteristics and construction of a structure

10._____ given to acts of violence or aggression

Guided Reading: *Fill in the blanks below to create complete sentences.*

1. Henry G. Bennett became the president of Oklahoma _____
College.

2. Bennett established a plan that was followed for more than _____ years
and helped make the university what it has become today.

3. George Lynn Cross oversaw a period of tremendous growth for the university as
_____ skyrocketed during the post-World War II era.

4. Carl Albert was a member of the House of Representatives for _____ years.

5. David Boren was a constant presence in Oklahoma _____
throughout the latter half of the 20th Century.

Matching: *Match the Oklahoma politician or university president with their significant accomplishments:*

a. Henry G. Bennett   c. Carl Albert
b. George Lynn Cross   d. David Boren

6._____ oversaw African American integration at the University of Oklahoma

7._____ helped establish an architectural style at Oklahoma State University that can
still be seen on campus today

8._____ reduced the state income tax and eliminated more than a hundred
government agencies

9._____ was Speaker of the House when Richard Nixon resigned the presidency

10._____ thirty-seven buildings were constructed at Oklahoma University while he was
president

Summarize: *Answer the following questions in the space provided. Attempt to respond in a complete sentence for each question. Be sure to use correct capitalization and punctuation!*

1. Who was Speaker of the House when Richard Nixon resigned the presidency?

2. What was Oklahoma State University once known as?

3. When was David Boren a U.S. Senator?

4. Where is there a statue of Henry Bennett today?

5. Why did Richard Nixon resign the presidency?

6. How did Henry Bennett have a lasting impact on Oklahoma State University?

Student Response: *Write a paragraph addressing the questions raised below. A thorough response should consist of three to five complete sentences.*

7. Carl Albert became the Speaker of the House in 1971. This is the highest ranking political position ever held by an Oklahoman. Why do you think it is so difficult for an Oklahoman to gain national political prominence?

Oklahoma has produced many well-known individuals throughout its history. Utilize a map of Oklahoma and internet resources to help you locate and label the following places mentioned in this unit.

Cities and towns should be labeled with a •

Chickasha (Ada Louis Sipuel & Bill Wallace)
Tahlequah (Jerome Tiger)
Savinaw (Mickey Mantle)
Henryetta (Troy Aikman)

Anadarko (Kiowa Six)
Pawnee (Chester Gould)
Binger (Johnny Bench)
Yukon (Garth Brooks)

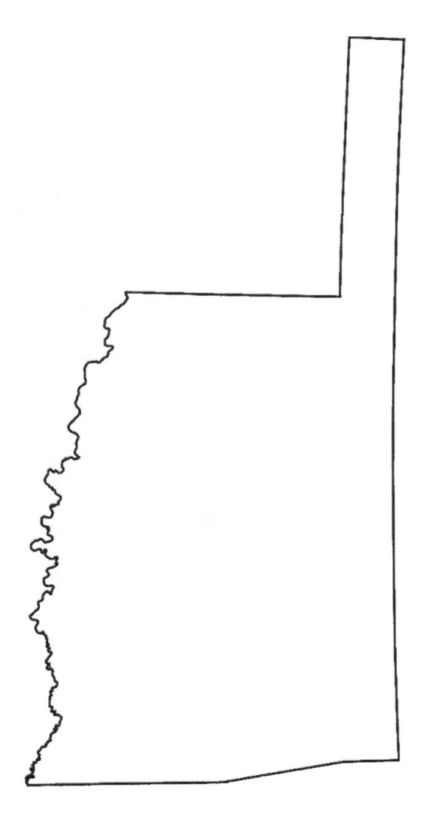

Unit Six:
Unique Oklahoma

Oklahoma Weather

The weather in Oklahoma is notoriously unpredictable. What types of weather does the state experience? Why does the weather fluctuate so often?

In general, the weather in Oklahoma varies widely from the southeastern portion of the state to the extreme western regions of the panhandle. The average temperature in the southeastern part of the state is 62°, while in the panhandle the average temperature is 58°. Rainfall varies as well. Some parts of the state receive as much as 56 inches of precipitation a year, while there are parts of the panhandle were it rains as little as 17 inches! In the winter, the southern region of the state gets as little as four inches of snow a year, while the northern part of the state can receive as much as twenty.

The Great Plains region of the country experiences unconventional weather because of the geography of North America. There is no mountain range running east to west in North America. This allows cold air coming from the Rocky Mountains to frequently collide with warm air coming from the Gulf of Mexico. The two meet over the Great Plains, causing weather patterns that tend to change frequently and with little anticipation.

Rapid temperature changes are to be expected, especially in the spring and in the fall. For example, on November 11, 1911, the temperature reached 83° in the afternoon. By midnight, the temperature had fallen 66°, reaching a low of 17°. This means that for the date of November 11, the record high and low temperatures both occurred on the exact same day!

Of course, the most extreme weather phenomenon created by the collision of warm air and cold air are violent thunderstorms and tornadoes. So many tornadoes occur in the Great Plains region that the area has earned the nickname "tornado alley". Oklahoma experiences an average of 62 tornadoes each year.

One of the most significant outbreaks of tornadoes happened not long after Oklahoma became a state. On April 27-28 of 1912, twenty-six tornadoes ripped through the state, six of which were extremely violent. At least fifteen cities were struck by the storms and forty deaths were recorded.

A deadly string of eight or nine tornadoes plagued the panhandle of Texas, western Oklahoma, and southern Kansas on April 9, 1947. The first tornado touched down near White Deer, Texas. The storm continued to track to the northeast, producing multiple vortexes as it went. The worst of these was an F-5 tornado which struck several towns in both Texas and Oklahoma. The storm was at its worst when it hit Woodward, Oklahoma. The tornado was two-miles wide and leveled 100 city blocks. The storm caused millions of dollars in damage in all three states, and 181 people lost their lives that day.

One of the largest tornadoes in the history of the U.S. occurred on May 3rd, 1999. At 301 mph, the storm set a record for the highest winds ever recorded on the face of the planet. It struck the town of Bridge Creek, Oklahoma before moving on to the much larger community of Moore. This tornado stayed on the ground for 85 minutes and traveled an astonishing 38 miles. More than 8,000 homes were destroyed and the storm caused over $1 billion in damages. This massive tornado was only one of more than 150 that touched down from May 2nd through May 8th of 1999.

Words to watch for

fluctuate

phenomenon

vortex

unconventional

May 20, 2013 saw another massive tornado hit Moore. The tornado had winds of more than 210 mph and was over a mile wide. Twenty-four people perished in the storm and hundreds were injured.

Oklahoma's weather can be very dangerous, and storms will surely continue to ravage the state. However, majestic sunsets, rhythmic rainfall, beautiful snowfall, and lightning-filled skies will also continue to fill Oklahomans with wonder.

Multiple Choice: *Select the choice that completes the statement or answers the question.*

1._____ Which of the following best identifies weather patterns in the state of Oklahoma?
a. The weather in Oklahoma varies widely from the southeastern portion of the state to the extreme western regions of the panhandle.
b. The weather in Oklahoma is surprisingly consistent from the southeastern portion of the state to the extreme western regions of the panhandle.
c. The weather in Oklahoma varies widely from the coastal portion of the state to the extreme interior.
d. The weather in Oklahoma varies widely from the Red River to the Canadian River.

2._____ Which of the following best describes the level of precipitation normally received in the Oklahoma panhandle?
a. The Oklahoma panhandle consistently receives about 56 inches of rain a year.
b. There are parts of the panhandle were it rains as little as 17 inches a year.
c. During the winter, the Oklahoma panhandle receives heavy amounts of rainfall.
d. The Oklahoma panhandle sometimes goes more than a decade without receiving any rainfall at all.

3._____ Which of the following best explains why Oklahoma experiences such unstable weather?
a. The air pressure caused by the rolling Great Plains create a very unstable environment.
b. Mountain ranges which run east to west in North America trap in and circulate high pressure air currents.
c. Cold air coming from the Rocky Mountains frequently collides with warm air coming from the Gulf of Mexico.
d. Warm air coming from the Rocky Mountains frequently collides with cold air coming from the Gulf of Mexico.

4._____ Which of the following is an opinion?
a. Tornadoes are created by the collision of warm air and cold air.
b. The Great Plains are known as "tornado alley".
c. Oklahoma experiences an average of 62 tornadoes a year.
d. In terms of weather, Oklahoma is the most dangerous place to live.

5._____ Which of the following statements is not true of the May 3, 1999 tornado that hit Moore, OK?
a. At 301 mph, the storm set a record for the highest winds ever recorded on the face of the planet.
b. This tornado stayed on the ground for 85 minutes and traveled an astonishing 38 miles.
c. More than 8,000 homes were destroyed and the storm caused more than $1 billion in damages.
d. The tornado was part a series of storms that killed 181 people in Texas, Oklahoma, and Kansas.

Vocabulary: *Match each word with its correct definition. Consider how the word is used in the lesson. This might help you define each term. Use a dictionary to help if necessary.*

a. fluctuate
b. unconventional
c. phenomenon

d. vortex
e. astonishing

6._____ something that is impressive or extraordinary

7._____ a whirling mass of air, especially one in the form of a visible column or spiral, as a tornado

8._____ to change continually; shift back and forth; vary irregularly

9._____ not bound by or conforming to convention, rule, or precedent

10._____ causing surprise; amazing

Name_____

Guided Reading: *Fill in the blanks below to create complete sentences.*

1. The weather in Oklahoma is notoriously _____.

2. The average temperature in the southeastern part of the state is 62°, while in the _____ the average temperature is 58°.

3. In the winter, the southern region of the state gets as little as _____ of snow a year.

4. The Great Plains region of the country typically experiences unconventional weather because of the unusual _____ of North America.

5. There is no mountain range running _____ in North America.

6. Rapid _____ changes are to be expected, especially in the spring and in the fall.

7. The most extreme weather phenomenon created by the collision of warm air and cold air are violent thunderstorms and _____.

8. So many tornadoes occur in the Great Plains region that the area has earned the nickname "_____".

9. The 1947 Woodward tornado was _____ and leveled 100 city blocks.

10. May 20, 2013 saw another massive tornado hit _____.

Summarize: *Answer the following questions in the space provided. Attempt to respond in a complete sentence for each question. Be sure to use correct capitalization and punctuation!*

1. Who consistently experiences the least amount of rain in Oklahoma?

2. What is unique about November 11, 1911?

3. When did a tornado destroy 100 city blocks of Woodward, Oklahoma?

4. Where is "tornado alley"?

5. Why does Oklahoma experience such unusual weather patterns?

6. How many people lost their lives during the April 9, 1947 tornado outbreak?

Student Response: *Write a paragraph addressing the questions raised below. A thorough response should consist of three to five complete sentences.*

7. Tornadoes have been common throughout the state's history, but far fewer lives are lost to tornadoes now than in the early days of statehood (despite many of the tornadoes being larger). Why do you believe this is the case? Explain your answer!

The University of Oklahoma

The state's flagship university is the University of Oklahoma. When was the university founded? What is it well-known for?

The University of Oklahoma (in Norman) was established in December of 1890 by the territorial legislature. It was originally known as Norman Territorial University and became the University of Oklahoma in 1907 when Oklahoma was admitted into the Union as the 46th state.

The university grew throughout the early half of the 20th Century, but experienced its most significant growth in the years following World War II. The 1950s and early 1960s saw not only a rapid rise in the student population of the university, but also the expansion of campus facilities as well. New dorms, classrooms, and other buildings were being constructed during that time.

The late 1940s and 1950s also saw other changes at the university. African American students such as Ada Lois Sipuel and George McLaurin challenged the University of Oklahoma in court. In both cases, the students were denied entry into the university because of their race; in both cases, the United States Supreme Court ruled that OU was required to allow the students into their graduate programs. As the decade of the 1950s progressed, other groundbreaking moments were achieved as integration continued. Prentice Gautt became the university's first African American football player in 1956.

Athletics has always been an important part of the University of Oklahoma. The school has consistently had one of the elite football programs in the nation. Its status as a football powerhouse was solidified in the 1950s with its legendary coach Bud Wilkinson. Wilkinson won 145 games as the Sooners' head coach as well as three national championships. Wilkinson's tenure also produced the record-setting 47 game win streak—a record which remains unbroken. The university has produced seven Heisman Trophy winners, and it is the only school with four coaches who have won more than 100 games (Bennie Owen, Bud Wilkinson, Barry Switzer, and Bob Stoops).

OU has been very successful in other sports as well. This success includes seven national championships in wrestling and five in gymnastics. The baseball and softball teams have also won national titles. The men's and women's basketball teams have also made multiple appearances in the "Final Four" of the NCAA championship basketball tournament.

There are several notable features on campus as well. The Museum of Art, founded in 1936, has more than 8,000 works of art. Many of these pieces were created by renowned Native American artists, but the display also includes works by Claude Monet, Pierre-August Renoir, and Vincent VanGogh.

The University of Oklahoma Library also has an impressive collection. The library boasts more than 4.7 million volumes. Amongst the more unique items it possesses are hand-written notes from Galileo Galilei and more than fifty books which were printed in the 15th Century! The library also has more than 1.5 million maps and 1.6 million photographs available for research purposes.

> *Words to watch for*
>
> union   flagship
>
> artifacts   doctorate

The Sam Noble Museum of Natural History was founded in 1899, and today it has more than 5 million artifacts. The focus of the museum is the history of the animals and people that have lived in the region that is now Oklahoma throughout its long history.

Today, the University of Oklahoma has over 30,000 students enrolled. It offers more than 150 different degree programs and 75 doctorate programs. There is no doubt that it will continue to be the state's featured university for many years to come.

Multiple Choice: *Select the choice that completes the statement or answers the question.*

1._____ Which of the following statements is *not* true?
a.   The University of Oklahoma was established in December of 1890 by the territorial legislature.
b.   The University of Oklahoma was originally known as Norman Territorial University.
c.   The university changed to its current name in 1907.
d.   The University of Oklahoma is the second-largest university in the state of Oklahoma.

2._____ Which of the following best describes the founding of the University of Oklahoma?
a.   The university was founded during territorial days, before Oklahoma became a state.
b.   The university was founded shortly after Oklahoma became a state.
c.   The university was founded during the Great Depression, as part of the New Deal.
d.   The university was founded shortly after World War II.

3._____ Which of the following did *not* occur at the University of Oklahoma during the 1950s?
a.   Some of the first African American students were admitted.
b.   The first African American football player took the field for the Sooners.
c.   The university changed its name.
d.   The school's status as a football powerhouse was solidified with its legendary coach Bud Wilkinson.

4._____ How was the University of Oklahoma's football program originally established as a powerhouse?
a.   During World War II, the Oklahoma Sooners enthralled the nation by winning 82 straight football games with their wide open passing attack.
b.   During the 1960s, the University of Oklahoma won seven conference championships and three straight national titles.
c.   During the 1950s, Coach Bud Wilkinson's Sooners won 145 games and three national championships.
d.   During the 1990s, the University of Oklahoma held the longest winning streak in all of college football.

5._____ Which of the following is true of the Sam Noble Museum of Natural History?
a.   The focus of the museum is the history of the animals and people that once inhabited Central America.
b.   The focus of the museum is the history of the animals and people that have lived in the region that is now Oklahoma.
c.   The focus of the museum is the history of Eastern Civilizations.
d.   The focus of the museum is the history of the culture of Western Civilization.

Vocabulary: *Match each word with its correct definition. Consider how the word is used in the lesson. This might help you define each term. Use a dictionary to help if necessary.*

a.   flagship
b.   Union
c.   facilities

d.   artifact
e.   doctorate

6._____ a single unit from a related group considered as the most important

7._____ something designed, built, installed, etc.

8._____ the United States

9._____ the highest academic degree in any field of knowledge

10._____ any object made by human beings, especially with a view to subsequent use

Name_____

Guided Reading: *Fill in the blanks below to create complete sentences.*

1. The state's _____ university is the University of Oklahoma.

2. The University of Oklahoma was established in December of 1890 by the _____.

3. The University of Oklahoma experienced its most significant growth in the years following _____.

4. African American students such as _____ and George McLaurin challenged the University of Oklahoma in court.

5. _____ became the university's first African American football player in 1956.

6. Bud Wilkinson's tenure as football coach produced the record-setting _____ game win streak—a record which remains unbroken.

7. The University of Oklahoma has produced seven _____ winners.

8. The men's and women's basketball teams have made multiple appearances in the "_____".

9. The _____, founded in 1936, has more than 8,000 works of art.

10. The University of Oklahoma Library possesses hand-written notes from _____.

Summarize: *Answer the following questions in the space provided. Attempt to respond in a complete sentence for each question. Be sure to use correct capitalization and punctuation!*

1. Who was OU's first African American football player?

2. What was the University of Oklahoma's original name?

3. When did the university become known as the University of Oklahoma?

4. Where is the University of Oklahoma's campus?

5. Why are the contents of the University of Oklahoma Library regarded as such an impressive collection?

6. How many students are currently enrolled at the University of Oklahoma?

Student Response: *Write a paragraph addressing the questions raised below. A thorough response should consist of three to five complete sentences.*

7. After reading about the University of Oklahoma, what aspect of the university are you most impressed with? Why?

©Reading Through History

Oklahoma State University

Oklahoma has several well-respected universities. One of these schools is Oklahoma State University. How long has the university existed? Has it always been known as Oklahoma State University?

Oklahoma State University was founded in 1890 as part of the Morrill Act which was a law passed by the US Congress. This act turned federally-controlled lands over to each state (or territory) so that the land could be sold by the state. In turn, the money would be used for the creation of public universities (these universities became known as land-grant colleges).

The school now known as Oklahoma State University was founded as Oklahoma Agricultural & Mechanical College. Throughout its first few years, Oklahoma A&M held its classes in church buildings until a proper campus could be constructed. Its first graduating class in 1896 included only six students.

The university grew rapidly throughout the first half of the 20th Century, and by 1957, many felt it had out-grown its name. Thus, Oklahoma A&M became Oklahoma State University of Agriculture and Applied Sciences. This name change reflected the larger variety of curriculum that was now being offered by the school. As the university continued to expand even more, the latter portion of this name was dropped, and the school became known as Oklahoma State University.

<table>
<tr><td>

Words to watch for

tradition   collectively

diverse   undergraduate

</td></tr>
</table>

The school has a rich and diverse tradition in athletics, excelling in many different sports throughout its existence. The Cowboys football team has produced a large number of players who went on to outstanding success in the professional ranks. Heisman Trophy winner Barry Sanders is regarded as one of the best running backs to ever play in the NFL, while Thurman Thomas played in four Super Bowls. Both stars are in the National Football Hall of Fame.

OSU's baseball team has also generated a large number of players who went on to success in Major League Baseball. Pete Incaviglia, Mickey Tettleton, Robin Ventura, and many others have made it to the big leagues.

OSU has experienced its greatest athletic success in golf and wrestling. Ricky Fowler, Scott Verplank, Charles Howell III, Bo Van Pelt, and Hunter Mahan were all standout golfers at OSU who went on to become professionals. The OSU golf team has won ten NCAA championships. The Cowboys' wrestling team has won an impressive 34 national titles. There have also been 55 Oklahoma State athletes compete in the Olympics in various sports. Collectively, these competitors won 21 gold medals.

Oklahoma State also has a very proud tradition in basketball. The men's basketball team has won two national championships (1945 & 1946). From 1934 to 1970, the team was coached by the legendary Henry Iba who amassed an impressive 755 wins throughout his career. To this day, OSU plays basketball in a facility which bears his name, Gallegher-Iba Arena.

The school has a Homecoming tradition which is nearly unrivaled across the nation. The festivities include a Harvest Carnival and the Sea of Orange Parade. It is billed as "America's Greatest Homecoming Celebration". It routinely brings in more than 70,000 alumni to enjoy the weekend.

Today, OSU's campus in Stillwater, Oklahoma has an enrollment of more than 20,000 students. There are nearly 200 undergraduate degree programs, with its premiere college being the College of Agricultural Sciences and Natural Resources. The future will almost certainly continue to be bright for the state's second largest university, as 2013 saw the school's largest freshman class ever!

*The numbers mentioned in this reading were accurate as of January 1, 2015.

Multiple Choice: *Select the choice that completes the statement or answers the question.*

1._____ Which of the following best describes the Morrill Act?
a.   This act placed a tax on federally-controlled land that could be used to fund the creation of public universities.
b.   This act turned federally-controlled lands over to each state (or territory) so that the land could be sold to fund the creation of public universities.
c.   This act mandated that each state create at least two public universities.
d.   This act set aside federally-controlled land in each state for the creation of public universities.

2._____ Which of the following best explains why the university changed its name in 1957?
a.   This name change reflected the larger variety of curriculum that was being offered by the school.
b.   Many felt that a name change would help the struggling university to attract more students.
c.   Many argued that their name was too similar to that of the University of Oklahoma.
d.   Many argued that there were too many Agricultural & Mechanical colleges in the state of Oklahoma.

3._____ Which of the following correctly identifies Hall of Fame football players who attended Oklahoma State University?
a.   Jerry Rice and Thurman Thomas
b.   Jim Kelly and Barry Sanders
c.   Jerry Rice and Jim Kelly
d.   Barry Sanders and Thurman Thomas

4._____ Which of the following correctly identifies the sports where Oklahoma State University has achieved the most success?
a.   football and wrestling   c.   golf and wrestling
b.   football and golf   d.   basketball and golf

5._____ Which of the following is *not* true of OSU's homecoming celebration?
a.   The festivities include a Harvest Carnival and the Sea of Orange Parade.
b.   The event is billed as "America's Greatest Homecoming Celebration".
c.   The Oklahoma State Cowboys always play either the Oklahoma Sooners or the Texas Longhorns as part of the event.
d.   It typically brings in more than 70,000 alumni to enjoy the weekend.

Vocabulary: *Match each word with its correct definition. Consider how the word is used in the lesson. This might help you define each term. Use a dictionary to help if necessary.*

a.   diverse   d.   tradition
b.   generated   e.   undergraduate
c.   collectively

6._____ of a different kind, form, character, etc.

7._____ a continuing pattern or practice

8._____ a student in a university or college who has not received a first, especially a bachelor's, degree

9._____ forming a whole; combined

10._____ to bring into existence; cause to be; produce

Guided Reading: *Fill in the blanks below to create complete sentences.*

1. Oklahoma State University was founded as part of the _____ which was a law passed by the US Congress.

2. The school now known as Oklahoma State University was founded as Oklahoma _____ College.

3. Throughout its first few years, Oklahoma A&M held its classes in _____ until a proper campus could be constructed.

4. The school has a rich and diverse tradition in _____, excelling in many different sports throughout its existence.

5. Heisman Trophy winner _____ is regarded as one of the best running backs to ever play in the NFL.

6. Pete Incaviglia, Mickey Tettleton, _____, and many others have made it to the big leagues.

7. The OSU golf team has won _____ NCAA championships.

8. The Cowboys' _____ team has won an impressive 34 national titles.

9. Collectively, Olympians who have attended Oklahoma State have won 21 _____.

10. The OSU men's basketball team has won two _____ (1945 & 1946).

Summarize: *Answer the following questions in the space provided. Attempt to respond in a complete sentence for each question. Be sure to use correct capitalization and punctuation!*

1. Who coached the Oklahoma State men's basketball team from 1934 to 1970?

2. What was the original name of Oklahoma State University?

3. When was Oklahoma State University founded?

4. Where is Oklahoma State University?

5. Why did the university change its name in 1957?

6. How many people were part of Oklahoma State's first graduating class?

Student Response: *Write a paragraph addressing the questions raised below. A thorough response should consist of three to five complete sentences.*

7. Why do you believe that Oklahoma thought it necessary to have an Agricultural & Mechanical college in addition to their state university? Explain your answer!

Enterprising Oklahoma Businesses

Oklahoma has produced many successful businesses throughout its brief history. What are some of the more prominent businesses that started in Oklahoma? Are those businesses still successful today?

On July 21, 1975, two graduates of Oklahoma State University, Stan Clark and Steve File, opened a bar close to the campus of their old college. They decided to name the establishment Eskimo Joe's. In 1984, the bar became a restaurant when hamburgers and other food items were added to the menu.

The restaurant has become famous for its merchandise. Eskimo Joe's T-shirts, featuring Eskimo Joe and his dog Buffy, have become some of the most frequently sold T-shirts in the world. The restaurant in Stillwater remains a popular hotspot for students at Oklahoma State University and has become one of the state's most enduring tourist attractions.

Braum's Ice Cream and Dairy Stores was founded in 1968 by Bill Braum and his wife Mary. They opened 24 stores in their first year and continued to grow from there. Initially, their products were brought from Emporia, Kansas, but in 1975, they moved their herd of dairy cows to Tuttle, Oklahoma. To this day, the dairy farm in Tuttle is the backbone of the empire.

Braum's controls every aspect of its products from the company's dairy farm, processing plants, and bakeries... even the packaging used in their restaurants is produced by Braum's. Products are shipped on Braum's trucks and delivered directly to each of their stores.

There are currently more than 250 Braum's locations throughout Oklahoma, Texas, Kansas, Arkansas, and Missouri. Each of these locations is less than 300 miles from the Braum's farm in Tuttle. This is done to ensure that all Braum's products remain fresh while in route to the store. Braum's also claims to be the only major ice cream maker to still milk its own cattle.

> **Words to watch for**
>
> prominent   establishment
>
> merchandise   entrepreneur

The fast-food drive-in chain of restaurants now known as Sonic got their start in 1953, in Shawnee, Oklahoma. Troy N. Smith Sr. was running a root beer stand, as well as a steak restaurant, with his business partner. The two men realized that they were making far more money off of the root beer stand (which also sold hamburgers and hotdogs), so they began to focus on this part of the business even more. They named their little stand Top Hat Drive-In.

The second Top Hat location was built in Woodward and restaurants in Enid and Stillwater soon followed. Before long, the Top Hat name was changed to Sonic, and the business quickly grew. Sonic has become well-known for its drive-in stalls and roller-skating car-hops.

Today (2015) there are more than 3,500 Sonic restaurants in 43 different states. They serve an estimated 3 million customers on a daily basis, and their headquarters can be found in Oklahoma City, Oklahoma.

There are many other successful businesses that operate in Oklahoma, and the state will certainly continue to be a place of entrepreneurs who are fueled by a pioneer spirit.

Name_____

Multiple Choice: *Select the choice that completes the statement or answers the question.*

1._____ Which of the following describes the founding of Eskimo Joe's?
a. In 1975, two graduates of Oklahoma State University opened a bar close to the campus of their old college.
b. In 1968, a couple opened a dairy business centered around their farm in Tuttle, Oklahoma.
c. In 1953, Troy Smith turned a popular root beer stand into a fast-food drive-in restaurant in Shawnee, Oklahoma.
d. In 1985, two graduates of the University of Oklahoma opened a bar close to the campus of their old college.

2._____ Which of the following best describes Braum's?
a. Braum's is a single restaurant in Tuttle, Oklahoma. They are famous for their chicken and cheese fries.
b. Braum's is a regional chain of ice cream and dairy stores.
c. Braum's is a chain of drive-in restaurants that is famous for their car-hops.
d. Braum's is a chain of supermarkets that stretches across the American Southwest.

3._____ Which of the following describes what makes Braum's so unique?
a. Despite selling so much merchandise, Braum's has remained a one site store.
b. Braum's displays an extensive collection of historical artifacts, mainly soda bottles, inside their restaurants.
c. The dairy cattle, processing plants, bakeries, and even the packaging used in their stores is owned and produced by Braum's.
d. Braum's has become quite famous for their unique T-shirts.

4._____ Which of the following correctly identifies the origin of the Sonic restaurant chain?
a. Sonic began as a bar near the OSU campus in Stillwater, Oklahoma.
b. Sonic began as a steakhouse in Woodward, Oklahoma.
c. Sonic began as a dairy farm in Emporia, Kansas.
d. Sonic began as a rootbeer stand known as Top Hat Drive-In in Shawnee, Oklahoma.

5._____ Which of the following statements is *not* true?
a. In 1984, Eskimo Joe's became a restaurant when hamburgers and other food items were added to the menu.
b. In 1975, the Braum family moved their herd of dairy cows to Tuttle, Oklahoma.
c. Sonic serves an estimated 3 million customers on a daily basis.
d. There are more than 250 Eskimo Joe's restaurants across the United States.

Vocabulary: *Match each word with its correct definition. Consider how the word is used in the lesson. This might help you define each term. Use a dictionary to help if necessary.*

a. prominent
b. establishment
c. merchandise
d. backbone
e. entrepreneur

6._____ the central or outstanding feature

7._____ a place of business together with its employees, merchandise, equipment, etc.

8._____ goods, especially manufactured goods; commodities

9._____ leading, important, or well-known

10._____ a person who organizes and manages any enterprise, especially a business, usually with considerable initiative and risk

Guided Reading: *Fill in the blanks below to create complete sentences.*

1. On July 21, 1975, two graduates of _____ opened a bar close to the campus of their college.

2. In 1984, _____ became a restaurant when hamburgers and other food items were added to the menu.

3. Eskimo Joe's has become famous for its _____.

4. Eskimo Joe's restaurant has become one of Oklahoma's most enduring _____.

5. Braum's Ice Cream and Dairy Stores was founded in _____.

6. In 1975, the Braum family moved their herd of dairy cows to _____, Oklahoma.

7. Each Braum's location is less than _____ miles from the family's farm in Tuttle.

8. The fast-food drive-in chain of restaurants now known as _____ got their start in 1953, in Shawnee, Oklahoma.

9. Sonic has become well-known for its drive-in stalls and roller-skating _____.

10. Sonic's headquarters can be found in _____, Oklahoma.

Summarize: *Answer the following questions in the space provided. Attempt to respond in a complete sentence for each question. Be sure to use correct capitalization and punctuation!*

1. Who founded Eskimo Joe's?

2. What was the original name of Sonic?

3. When was Braum's founded?

4. Where is Eskimo Joe's?

5. Why has Braum's limited its expansion to a regional level?

6. How many Sonics were there in early 2015?

Student Response: *Write a paragraph addressing the questions raised below. A thorough response should consist of three to five complete sentences.*

7. Of the businesses mentioned in this lesson, only Eskimo Joe's determined to remain a one site restaurant. Why do you suppose this is the case? What other elements about the establishment stand out as being unique?

Oklahoma Astronauts

The state of Oklahoma has produced many astronauts over the years. Who were some of these astronauts? Which missions did they participate in?

Oklahoma's first astronaut was Gordon Cooper from Shawnee, Oklahoma. Cooper enlisted in the U.S. Marine Corps as a young man, but eventually transferred to the Air Force. He earned a degree in Aerospace Engineering in 1956 and was assigned to be a test pilot at Edwards Air Force Base in California. Just after the creation of the National Aeronautics and Space Administration (NASA), Cooper was one of 109 pilots chosen to take part in the selection process to become a part of Project Mercury. Cooper was the youngest of the seven men chosen to be NASA's first astronauts.

On May 15, 1963, Cooper launched into space aboard Mercury-Atlas 9. He orbited the Earth 22 times, traveling more than 500,000 miles. During that time, he also became the first American to sleep while in space. Cooper returned to space a second time onboard Gemini 5. He eventually retired from NASA having logged 222 hours in space. His early career in NASA has been depicted in the motion picture *The Right Stuff*.

Tom Stafford, from Weatherford, Oklahoma, graduated from the U.S. Naval Academy in 1952. In 1962, Stafford was chosen as one of NASA's second group of astronauts. He was chosen to participate in both the Gemini and Apollo projects. Stafford entered space in December of 1965 as part of the crew of Gemini VI. He returned to space as the commander of the Gemini IX mission in 1966.

Tom Stafford

In May of 1969, Stafford commanded the Apollo 10 mission. This mission was essentially a dress-rehearsal for the moon landing which would occur during the Apollo 11 flight. The Apollo 10 crew performed every part of the moon landing procedure, with the exception of actually landing on the moon.

Words to watch for:
orbit   demonstration
elite   biochemistry

Stafford eventually became the Deputy Director of Flight Crew Operations for NASA. He rose to the rank of lieutenant general before retiring from the Air Force in 1979. In 1990, he assisted NASA in developing a plan for the next thirty years of space flight.

William Pogue, a Choctaw from Okemah, Oklahoma, enlisted in the Air Force in 1951. In 1955, he became a member of the Thunderbirds, the Air Force's elite aerial demonstration team. He was selected as an astronaut in 1966. Pogue traveled into space as the pilot of the Skylab 4 mission. This was the last of the manned missions to the Skylab space station. During this mission, he and his fellow astronauts completed more than fifty experiments and more than twenty scientific demonstrations.

Owen K. Garriott was born and raised in Enid, Oklahoma. He received a bachelor's degree in Electrical Engineering from the University of Oklahoma before joining the Navy in 1953. He also earned a PhD in Electrical Engineering from Stanford University in 1960.

Garriott was selected as one of six scientist-astronauts in 1965. He first went to space as part of the Skylab 3 mission in 1973. As part of this mission, he and his fellow astronauts conducted a wide variety of experiments on the sun. Garriott also established a new record, staying in space for 60 days. This was more than twice the length of the previous record. Garriott returned to space ten years later aboard space shuttle *Columbia*.

Shannon Lucid

Shannon Lucid was raised in Bethany, Oklahoma. She earned a PhD in biochemistry from the University of Oklahoma in 1973. Lucid was selected for astronaut training in 1978, one of the first six women selected for such training.

Lucid first traveled into space onboard space shuttle *Discovery* in 1985. She returned to space in 1989, 1991, and 1993. In 1996, Lucid spent 188 days aboard the Mir space station. This lengthy stay established two records. She had spent more time in orbit than any other American and more time in space than any other female. In 2003, Lucid became NASA's Chief Scientist, and in 2014 she was selected to the United States Astronaut Hall of Fame.

From the era of the land run through the space age, Oklahomans have always had a pioneer spirit. There is little doubt that future Oklahomans will continue shooting for the stars.

Multiple Choice: *Select the choice that completes the statement or answers the question.*

1._____ Which of the following is *not* true about Gordon Cooper?
a. Cooper was one of NASA's first seven astronauts.
b. Cooper entered space aboard Mercury-Atlas 9.
c. Cooper became the youngest man to walk on the moon.
d. Cooper's early career at NASA is depicted in the film *The Right Stuff*.

2._____ Which of the following made Tom Stafford's mission aboard Apollo 10 significant?
a. The Apollo 10 mission was the first moon landing.
b. The Apollo 10 mission was a rehearsal for the moon landing.
c. The Apollo 10 mission was the first manned mission into space.
d. The Apollo 10 mission resulted in the first American deaths in space.

3._____ Which of the following statements about William Pogue is *not* accurate?
a. Pogue was a member of the Thunderbirds.
b. Pogue became an astronaut in 1966.
c. Pogue was a member of the last manned mission to Skylab.
d. Pogue personally conducted more than fifty experiments aboard Skylab.

4._____ Which of the following statements about Owen K. Garriott is true?
a. Garriott was from Enid, Oklahoma.
b. Garriott first went into space as part of the Skylab 3 mission.
c. Garriott established a record, spending more than 100 days in space.
d. Garriott returned to space aboard the space shuttle *Columbia*.

5._____ Which of the following is probably the most significant fact about Shannon Lucid's career at NASA?
a. Lucid was selected for astronaut training in 1978.
b. Lucid first traveled into space aboard the space shuttle *Discovery*.
c. Lucid stayed in space for 188 days aboard the Mir space station.
d. Lucid was inducted into the United States Astronaut Hall of Fame in 2014.

Vocabulary: *Match each word with its correct definition. Consider how the word is used in the lesson. This might help you define each term. Use a dictionary to help if necessary.*

a. orbit
b. rehearsal
c. elite
d. demonstration
e. biochemistry

6._____ a practice, usually in preparation for performance

7._____ the curved path followed by a satellite around a sun or planet

8._____ a science dealing with the chemistry of living matter

9._____ the very best of a group or class

10. _____ a public exhibition

Guided Reading: *Fill in the blanks below to create complete sentences.*

1. Gordon Cooper was the youngest of the seven men chosen to be NASA's first _____.

2. Cooper orbited the Earth 22 times, traveling more than _____ miles.

3. Tom Stafford returned to space as the commander of the _____ mission in 1966.

4. The Apollo 10 crew performed every part of the moon landing procedure, with the exception of actually _____ on the moon.

5. Stafford eventually became the Deputy _____ of Flight Crew Operations for NASA.

6. William Pogue, a _____ from Okemah, Oklahoma, enlisted in the Air Force in 1951.

7. Owen K. Garriott earned a PhD in Electrical Engineering from _____ University in 1960.

8. Garriott first went to space as part of the _____ mission in 1973.

9. Shannon Lucid was one of the first six _____ selected for astronaut training.

10. Lucid spent more time in orbit than any other _____ and more time in space than any female.

Summarize: *Answer the following questions in the space provided. Attempt to respond in a complete sentence for each question. Be sure to use correct capitalization and punctuation!*

1. Whose early career with NASA is depicted in the film *The Right Stuff*?

2. What did Owen K. Garriott earn his PhD in?

3. When did the Apollo 10 mission take place?

4. Where was William Pogue from?

5. Why was Shannon Lucid's selection as an astronaut significant?

6. How many hours had Gordon Cooper spent in space at the time of his retirement?

Student Response: *Write a paragraph addressing the questions raised below. A thorough response should consist of three to five complete sentences.*

7. In your opinion, which of Oklahoma's astronauts was the most accomplished? Support your answer using details from the lesson you have just read. Be as thorough as possible.

Use the lessons included in this unit to help you answer the following questions.

1. _____ was the birthplace of Gordon Cooper, as well as the location of the first Sonic.

2. Tom Stafford was from _____, Oklahoma.

3. William Pogue was a Cherokee from _____, Oklahoma.

4. _____, Oklahoma was the birthplace of Owen K. Garriott.

5. Shannon Lucid was raised in _____, Oklahoma.

6. _____, Oklahoma is the home of both Eskimo Joe's and Oklahoma State University.

7. The University of Oklahoma can be found in _____, Oklahoma.

8. The headquarters for Braum's Ice Cream & Dairy is located in _____, Oklahoma.

Utilize a map of Oklahoma or internet resources to help you locate and label the cities mentioned above.

Cities and towns should be labeled with a •

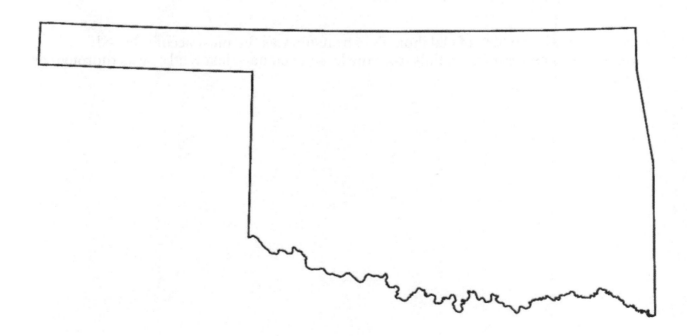

Made in the USA
Coppell, TX
25 June 2024

33905759R00090